New and Selected Poems
Munaldjali, Mutuerja

LIONEL FOGARTY has b... and important voice to emerge from a ... of Aboriginal writers. His poetry is written in the unique and highly rhythmic form of English that is the day-to-day language for many of the Murri tribes in Queensland, and puts the reader in touch with the spirituality of Murri culture and the raw realities of the Aborigines' struggle for self-determination and justice.

Lionel was born on the land of the Wakka Wakka tribe at Barambah, Queensland, which is now known as the Cherbourg Aboriginal Reserve. This was one of the 'punishment reserves' where individuals and their families who spoke out against the white authorities were sent from all over Queensland. As a result, the Wakka Wakka area became a place of many people from many different tribes.

With little formal education, Lionel left the Reserve at the age of sixteen and worked as a ring-barker, a railway worker and cleaner. At the same time, he became deeply involved with the Aboriginal struggle for land rights and justice. His poetry grew out of a commitment both to the Aboriginal cause and also a desire to communicate the traditional ways and beliefs of his community, which he has never deserted.

His first work of poetry, *Kargun*, was published when he was only twenty-two and was noted for the freshness and immediacy of his language. Over the years, his writing has been informed by a wealth of experience both as an activist, tribal member and a father. Although he has now published six books of poetry, he regards himself as a 'speaker' rather than a 'writer'.

He has travelled extensively, acting as an ambassador both for his Murri culture and the Aboriginal cause, throughout Australia, the U.S.A. and Europe (where his poetry is held in high regard). Most recently, he completed an exhaustive reading tour of Europe as part of the 1993 International Year for Indigenous Peoples, and has published, with the approval of his tribal elders, a traditional Wakka Wakka story, *Booyooburra*.

Also by Lionel Fogarty:

Poetry
Kargun (1980)
Yoogum Yoogum (1982)
Kudjela (1983)
Ngutji (1984)
Jagera (1990)

For Children
Booyooburra: A Tale of the Wakka Murri
illustrated by Sharon Hodgson,
(Hyland House, 1993)

New and Selected Poems

Munaldjali, Mutuerjaraera

Lionel G. Fogarty

This collection first published in 1995 by
Hyland House Publishing Pty Limited
(ACN 005 268 208)
'Hyland House'
387–389 Clarendon Street
South Melbourne, Victoria 3205

© Lionel G. Fogarty 1995

This book is copyright. Apart from any fair dealing for the purposes of private study, research, criticism or review, as permitted under the Copyright Act, no part may be reproduced by any process without written permission. Enquiries should be addressed to the publisher.

Publication of this title was assisted by the Commonwealth Government through the Australia Council, its arts funding and advisory body.

The author wishes to thank the following artists for the use of their materials:
Mike Jackson
Rose Bygraves
Rocko Langton
Garnet Mickelo
Daniel Yock
Charles Chambers (cover photograph)

National Library of Australia
Cataloguing-in-publication data:

Fogarty, Lionel George
  New and selected poems: munaldjali, mutuerjaraera.

  Includes index,
  ISBN 1 875657 18 5.

  1. Aborigines, Australian – Poetry. I. Title
A821.3

Typeset by Abb-typesetting Pty Ltd, Collingwood, Victoria
Printed in Australia by Brown Prior Anderson

Contents

BREAKING DOWN THE BARRIERS: ix
Introduction by Lionel Fogarty
GUERRILLA POETRY: xi
Foreword by Mudrooroo

NEW POEMS (1994)

For Him I Died — Bupu Ngunda I Love	3
Murra Murra Gulandanilli (Waterhen)	5
Imarbara I am — Generation of Existence	7
The Mununjali Exemption Man	8
Black Woman	9
A Vera Take a Ride	10
Joowindoo Goonduhmu	12
Quick sing (Translation)	13
Fellow being	14
Uppu Gulung Goowe (Good by and by)	15
Am I	16
The Children	17
Consideration of Black Deaths (story)	18
Rae Shines in Rivers	24
Come Over Murri	25
Memo to Us (story)	26
Yindingie Will Return Yenningee (story)	28
Sue and Du (The spirit of one tribe is all)	30
I'm Not Santa	32
Frisky Poem and Risky	34
Just Woke Up	36
Poem in Binga to You	37
Weather Comes	38
She Sang	39
Farewell Reverberated Vault of Detentions	40
Little Murri (Be a Murri before an Australian)	42
Drunk Cricket Field No. 1	44
Where Have You Been	47
Surviving Dreaming Surviving	48

from *Jagera* (1990)

Love	51
Mad Souls	52
Boundless Guides	53

For I Come . . . Death in Custody	54
For Aussie Mates of Natives	55
Ngunda . . . The God	56
Kath Walker	57
Bungoo Bungoo	58
'Dulpai — Ila Ngari Kim Mo-Man'	60

from *Ngutji* (1984)

The Buzz	69
Fuck All Departments	70
Love or Human Nature	72
Ngunda Man Koori	73
Fuck Off	75
Observable	76
Biral Codes	77
Indigenous Versus	78
Spirits Inscriptions: Toleration	79
Remember Something Like This	80
Delightful	83
Dreamtime	84

from *Kudjela* (1983)

Biral Biral	87
Disguised, Not Attitude	89
By Accident, Blinked	91
White Tendency	92
Jukambe Spirit — For the Lost	94
Lone Meditation	95
Ain't No Abo Way of Communication	96
Ode: Renewing to Spiritless	99
Scenic Wonders — We Nulla Fellas	100
Shadow of Yesterday	102
Kudjela — With My People, Always	103
Mulinjari	104
Big 'N' Riddle	105

from *Yoogum Yoogum* (1982)

Tired of Writing	109
The Worker Who, The Human Who, The Abo Who	110
At Home: To: Musgrave Park People	113
Sadness in Children	117
Damper Lingo: Don't Hold Back	118
For Youse	120
Balance of Nature	121
Free Our Dreams	122
Rainbow People and Human People	123

from *Kargun* (1980)
   Puzzled   129
   A Lie   130
   Blackfella Drunk, Blackfella Fights   131
   To Dundalli   132
   Are there Abo Schools?   133
   Mr Professor   134
   My Cry is Lost in a Name   135
   I am Black, I am Both You and I, Truganini   136
   Urban Black   137
   Ringbarking — the Contract Killers   138
   Moved Me   140
   Stranger in Cherbourg Once Knew   141
   You Who May Read My Words   142
   Capitalism — The Murderer in Disguise   144

Glossary   147

Index of First Lines   149

On Reading Lionel's Poems.

The sweeping of Murri decades,
Koori, Nyungar, all Us Mobs before and beyond.
His voice echoing, singing out the ages,
Present and past, his words singing
Shining from the pages.
Lionel takes our lives into his mouth,
Spits them out, crying with our needs,
Our desires, our wants and triumphs.
A true kuta to us all,
His words singing of love and hate.
Trespass not on us, our lands.

We need his voice, we need his words;
We need to read, break-dance into our cultures,
Treasures in the warga of the earth;
In the love-womb of our earth.
Aye, you listen in awe to Lionel's magic
Words, poems, songs, singing of our deeds,
His deeds, our seedlings growing from the earth
   mother.
Moorditj yida, kuta; moorditj yida, kuta.

Mudrooroo, 24 November 1994.

BREAKING DOWN THE BARRIERS

I want to give everybody my understanding so that they can understand what the reality is in my community; the dreaming and the need for a revival of my language and connection to the land.

When people read my poetry I want them to feel the spirit that is in me and in the people of my community.

You have to understand all the poetry I write in order to get the message. It's a performance in literary oral tradition, of even using their English against the English. The way they write and talk is ungrammatical, because it doesn't have any meanings in their spirit. More so, the cultural symbols that belong to my people are more significant to my people than the A, B and C. What I want to achieve in my writing one day is to put Aboriginal designs of art inside the lettering to bring a broader understanding to the meanings of the text.

This will break down the sophistication of black intellectual authors. My writing is to give a direction to Aboriginal people coming up in the future, to stay away from European colonialist ways of writing, and the disease of stupidity in their language. I want to use a method encouraging the readers to accept that the solitary Aborigines write to give spiritual and political understanding of the conventional social structure of their community.

I must say I think it's going to be difficult to divide the layout of my brain to you, but I have done it quite successfully in giving verses of text in a foreign tongue. I believe in the pride and heritage of an indigenous, ancestral past and future where the technicalities of written words can be broken down. I see words beyond any acceptable meaning, this is how I express my dreaming.

To Aboriginal people in my country, listening and hearing is more important than reading materials. The whole magical way of song and dance is difficult to write down very well, because poetry is emotion. Only a black writer can produce the authenticity in it. I don't believe that white writers can catch the intelligence or the meanness of the black guerrilla fighters (Jantamarra, Mulbaggarra, Dundalee and Pemulwuy, for example). Only we can bring out on paper what our fighters back then fought to produce, the raising of people's consciousness about what really happened back then.

In my writing I don't believe in compromise at all. I don't want to be a reconciliation writer or a reformist writer. I like to hit psychological minds and cross boundaries. It doesn't matter if it is in correct grammar or their style of writing, because the white man will always criticise written pieces of paper.

White man will never really fully interpret what a black man is thinking when he is writing. Maybe in the generations to come this may change.

There are many contradictions in European written material, but don't get confused with my negating the reality of literary white Australia. I know how white Australians write and I know how they talk. They'll never come near the fourth world. White man will never know — and the only way they will know is through Aboriginal tongues that dominate in our lingo. Aboriginal writers are the best writers to edit themselves and encapsulate the spirit of anger, to transform a good spirit.

Lionel Fogarty

This book is dedicated to my children Fletcher Campbell Lacey and Bart Willoughby (the most original indigenous muso).

GUERRILLA POETRY:
Lionel Fogarty's Response to Language Genocide

'Every colonised people — in other words, every people in whose soul an inferiority complex has been created by the death and burial of its local cultural originality — finds itself face to face with the language of the civilising nation ...' Franz Fanon

What happened to the Aboriginal languages of Australia? The English invader sought to destroy them utterly. The native was to be forced into the state of English civilisation, and this meant the death and destruction of Aboriginal language and culture. In the settled areas there was imposed a deliberate policy of language genocide, and in a few decades Aboriginal languages became broken collections of words falling haplessly into English language structures of varying degrees of worth — from the invader's viewpoint! This forced adoption of a foreign language was in itself judged from the view of European tradition riddled with class and racial prejudice. Kriol and Pidgin became objects of scholarly study and Aboriginal writers in English were criticised on their use of English and Aboriginal remnant words. What would be the Aboriginal response to this cultural and genocide imperialism, and who would make this response?

Lionel Fogarty refuses to surrender to the critical norms forced upon poets in Australia. He writes in a manner which is the response of an Aboriginal songman against the genocide inflicted on his language and the tyranny imposed on him by a foreign language. It is impossssible to read Lionel without realising that he is Black; it is impossible to read him and not realise the crimes committed against the Aboriginal people, and it is impossible to read him and not realise that here is a poet using the English language in a unique and new way. He wields a black pen, and writes a language reflecting the mixture the Aboriginal cultures have become in such concentration camps as Cherbourg, where the invader language was forced on the people. He uses that language in an effort to tear down the language structures which have been imposed on him and his people.

I would like to stress that Lionel does not rely on European models for his poetry, and that it is his genius which shapes his verse. He was born a victim in a world in which he and his people had no say. In Franz Fanon's sense he (and his people) was the native Other contrasted with the coloniser subject which sought to destroy the blackness within him, to render him as object into a subject reflecting the coloniser. In the coloniser's world the only subject to aspire to be was that of the coloniser, and the native object was seen as a coming-to-be subject fashioned on the British model. Generations of white Cherbourg managers tried to force his people, fashioning white masks for their black skins. They tried to force Lionel to don such a mask and the only result was the coming-to-be of Lionel Fogarty the poet whose genius born from the struggle gave birth to a new style, or system, of poetry drawing from a myriad of influences to forge an essential quintessence of Aboriginality. Here was no ersatz Bourgeois black in white face, but an Aboriginal man, a poet guerrilla using the language of the invader in an effort to smash open its shell and spill it open for poetic expression.

Lionel's poetry is moral to an extreme and brooks no opposition. It may be argued that victims of oppression have this extreme morality because they know what it is like to be on the receiving end of immorality, or an amorality masquerading as altruism.

If Lionel Fogarty rejects European models in his poetry, we may ask what models does he utilise? We know that English poetics touched him less than Afro-American songs, less than incidents of his life, in his Aboriginality, in Aboriginal history and in the deep and abiding white oppression which necessitated a referendum to bring Aboriginal people into the human race.

Lionel's poems are not derived from books but from life as lived in Australia and the world. His response to life creates not only his models but his words. Aboriginal writers without exception are committed writers. They are in no sense 'closet' writers of the Kafka ilk who see the world from the confines of a garret. The garret of Aborigines was provided by the English and once freed from it, they have no desire to isolate themselves from kith and kin. Lionel Fogarty was born in the garret of Cherbourg and what this means may be gleaned from a reading of the Queensland Acts governing Aborigines and also the rules and regulations of these so-called settlements. He was born under the heel of the oppressor and this has affected his view of the world as well as his poetry.

Everyone who has heard Lionel speak has found it a deeply moving experience. He is perhaps the best Aboriginal speaker I have heard, and it was of little wonder that in his first speaking before an audience, he came through.

Lionel's poetry has a sweep of style and a breadth of content which no other poet in Australia can match. His style is all his own and sometimes he writes in a simple style akin to the poems of Jack Davis and Kath Walker. These poems are open in meaning and sentiment to all, but especially in his later poetry, he excels as a guerrilla poet wielding the language of the invader in an urge to destroy that imposition and recreate a new language freed of restrictions and erupting a multi-meaning of ambiguity. This hints at the many possibilities of meaning in a feeling language freed from the intellectual dreariness of academic verse. In fact his use of language reminds us of the Indian theory of Rasa rather than the dried out theories of the head people who demolish poetry in their quest for intellectual understanding and not heart understanding.

When we read verses of Lionel's we appear to be in the presence of an anti-language which may appear meaningless if we seek for intellectual understanding, and fail to understand that we are confronted by groups of feeling-images rooted deep within the Aboriginal psyche and experience. And we may well be in the presence of an anti-poetry, a turning away of all that the critics hold dear, and in which even the rhythms are flattened out, sometimes changed abruptly, often discarded so that no sweet victory is held out to entice the reader who must grasp an entirety of feeling structure beyond dictionary meaning.

Lionel's poems are exceedingly complex and far from those nineteenth-century models said to be favoured by other Aboriginal poets. Lionel is different in that he is attempting to push meaning and at least the structure of the English language towards an absolute end and liberate his language from that cultural imperialism of the spirit imposed on him at Cherbourg. He is aware that the English language in which he writes is not really his own, but a thing apart from him, but the feeling is his, as are the Aboriginal words scattered throughout his texts which reveal that here is no Gubba writing, but a Murri able to use the language of the oppressor as a weapon captured from the enemy. He is Fanon's native, but he has not been assimilated into the language of the coloniser. He has captured it in a guerrilla action and made it over into a free one of the Aboriginal spirit.

Mudrooroo

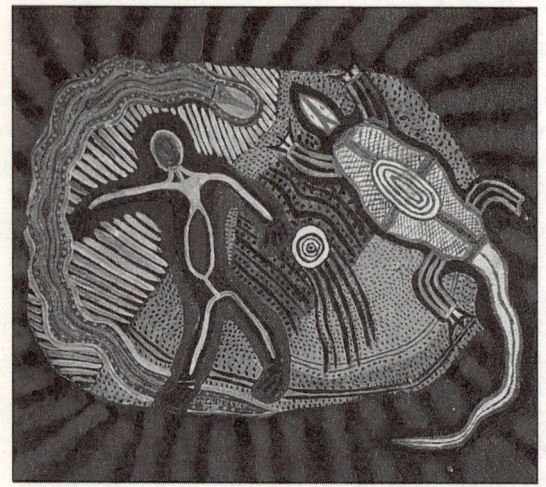

Daniel Yock

Air

Walk on my own
Talk on my own
Voice I hear
Steps I hear

Alone I see
Alone I hear
Alone my own

I give to poor
I give to receive
I give my last

Love is my pride
Love is a strong word
Love strong. Love lost

Daniel Yock 28/4/93

New Poems

Dedicated to Daniel Yock (Murra Murra Gulandanilli)
Born 7 February 1975. Died 7 November 1993

Mike Jackson

For Him I Died — Bupu Ngunda I Love

For him I loved
For him I became a dove
For him I tamed a game
Why has he taken my love
Wine as shaking my dine
Woe who outer my dinner room
What great sound he calls
What graving sound it gave
Wrap sapping his heart
With dem he got sung
For him I loved
Forgive the tearing
four faces he has seen
Funk hunk drunk
For him I lived He been in a body
I been in a bottler
Since once he send
Sin onto me
Now sinly I surrender
Sewer poorfully I adore
For him I loved Swear back just to glad
sweet birds just to grand
sweeping fights just to game
a one lone feels his sex
a two cone feeds his senses
a three owns feasts his sick
For him I loved
his silence liniment myths
his sires searcher meek in me
his resting bees many inner tests
even I forward his happy wills
even I forever his papa ills
even I forever his everlasting tills
For him I loved.
He bin in behind my soul
He bin in beloved mindness

He bin in beggar meanness
Why has he taken my lying
Win who in the taken winds
Will be bless my love my love giving
For him I love For him I loved
What great sound he calls calls

Rose Bygraves

Murra Murra Gulandanilli
Waterhen

Yet I too bleed the Murra Murra Gulandanilli heart
We blessed his body touched
We slipped to the earth feel with Daniel
I stepped proud, yielded dance
That was denial
My radical grumble with him
Oh man oh man
Him smiling at you,
Him a-laughing at you
Him eyes are dillil
Him understood the street lies
Him undertook eight and was mistook
Murra Murra Gulandanilli
Pain and ache
Yet he was loved by the Great Ones
Grief came out, out of sharing
And sharing and sharing alike was him
I still to this day feel
Danny Yock's consistency
The fate him kept
Paradise him kept
Dayock is a-calling contempt
To evil policies
Dayock is a-singing to the souls
Aborigine revolution coming
To those pigs sneer and judges too
Dayock want all you young to fight on
Not lurk on
To fight on To defend him
Dayock fear nobody
Cos him was a spiritual dancer
Was a Murra Murra dancer
Everybody praise within his respects
A distant happier came for a far a-wide
A-wide

Just a-greet Danny Yock
I asked a light of life and people
Here to 'member
The ember of the human spirit
To make him our brother Daniel dance that dance
Of the bleeding Murra Murra heart
He was taken away, taken away from me
in my heart living in always
The journey of his beginning
No more pain no more suffering
Dreamtime dancer keep me strong
Murra Murra Gulandanilli
Culture romancer
You're on the other side, the light you see
The light you see is where you're from
Is where you're going to be the from of the feeling that was
 within you
Can't you forget
Can't you remember
As long as I am a-grieving
You'll see justice will be done
Baba Yubbu
I will love you always
Your blood runs through me
I'll survive, we'll sunrise the enemy
At Murra Murra Gulandanilli dancer
The culture romancer
In my heart you're living always
In a Murri way of dancing
Dreamtime dancers
Romancers dance
Murra Murra Gulandanilli
Waterhen Waterhen Waterhen

Imarbara I am — Generation of Existence

I am a living entity, you belong to me. I AM.
I am of earth and space
I am a son of the world
I am the religious law
I am the kin to all creatures
I am kin to this creation
The world is my nation
The earth is my mother
The black man is of this earth
The red man is of this earth
And the yellow man of this earth
But where is the white mad man's home
He has rape in mind to his own mother earth
I have to fight with the trees
I have to fight with the rivers and rocks
Dear mother earth have my love
Day by day
Withdraw the force a companion pain of you, to be part of me
Please mother I'm sorry and lonely for your natural cause.
I am the birds dat die
I am the snakes dat die
I am the sea creatures to die
Sure man, we are but why must we bang and blast here on this
　　ground?
I'm your native here in captive
I'm your native ready in revolt
I'm the native to bring all
white human being to a new world
where you mother earth rule.
I know you can just take so much.
So I'm the land's sources of identity.
You mother earth provides for my physical needs
and my spiritual needs.
You are the holy and sacred and I'm the regeneration
of history and the continuation of your life
I'm the begin and dat where we all returns.

The Mununjali Exemption Man To my Great Grandfather Fred Fogarty

The Department of Family Services and Abos lied to me. My grandfather came to Purga at 'bout 19 or 18 hundreds and married a Murri woman who gave him sons. In 1922 he was given exemption certificate from the acts. He came from Mununjali people who lives in Beaudesert. My grandfather was gammin and told he was free, but when his son hit the manager his son was sended to Barambah.

Now my two grandfathers are dead and my parents can't remember any things they said or done cause in those days it was hard to tell.

So all I want to know is who was my great-great-great-grandfather's parents? Now some of these good christians must have paper records.

You see brothers and sisters I don't need whiteman papers to prove, but I want it to fight for legal — our land and cultural heritage rights.

Purga my grandparents help built, now is not ours. Well look at the mixed up mess.

Oh great grandfather I can't hear your yarning 'bout our relations Oh great grandfather I have your grandchildren ready to take up the fight for our land and losted you were taken and I'm lacking, so why don't we all come together as a family and re-issue free knowledge. Now my great grandfather was an aboriginal man dat is divide from me cos the history has changed camps. But I have moved too, yet I have a marriage certificate to you great-great-grandfather, and I will find you waiting in Mununjali Dreaming realities.

Black Woman

She's native, naked, she's native and naked
She takes me down and wipes my body
She holds me in her arms and warms my heart
She pushes into my mouth with the smell from future voices
She multitudes my soul into many magnificent beliefs
She never is betrayal to love
Ain't no mountain fireplace gonna encounter her burnt scar
Ain't tip-toe intense kiss gonna undress her lips
She has powers in dignity and her nights endure my feelings
    with the moon or stars
She turned my life's passions too beautifully for sleeping
    whispering
Glory travels worthy in her lyric spirit
I am fragile in mine but she comes in galaxy memorised
Some outrageous reality remains in this society, but she comes
    down plundering moves by radio hateness
She has been disappearing
She has been re-appearing
She is the spice of earth and is the psalm's privatisation
Tangled up in flesh matters my embracements are mine
Branches are of a thing now called gulls of agony
But she takes this over bridges
But she has private hurts and loves
Now my body speaking for everything she gave is spoken
But my robbed yearning became strangehood
But I praise her touch happenings in her stages.
She is my friend I sort of love her
But sick as me I believe in her returns.

A Vera Take a Ride

We use to ride emus and dolphins
We now have feathers over our bodys
You in black and me in red
inside a yellow man's dream
start us up we'll never stop
Gonna pump up your sense
Gonna rub in the juice
Is it any black wonder
Is it any white wonder
Trouble and strife making love
They fuss crazies and screaming
neighbours unto strangers
We used to ride emus and dolphins
You've wrecked our living
washing up, drinking, dancing
in engaging struggle, at didgeridoo groaning and straining
You made a grown race cry
You made a grown hate tearer
some are lazy slobs
some are marrying speed
now mean mean machine
open your heart starter
We shine out in the sun
We living scared in being shined
You gotta feel to love
shock dem, sink dem
We are brothers in our own
adolescence maybe cold running
You know chain and reality
now quotes of conversations
come once on a noise breeze
like echoes in the name of
guerrillas in another range

We ride the emu fast
We speak to dolphins for us to ride
when we win the ministry
don't come wondering about
We used to sing martyrs to the harvest
of the leaving fruit
Just circulate passion surrendered
in our consolation of action
ride dat dolphins and emus faster.

Joowindoo Goonduhmu

Ngujoo nye muyunube
Little black buree
You must respect golo
You must praise to junun
You must seek love with googee
little black buree hear your
song 'nuyeeree munu juwoon'
The gendergender
will bring the message
The googuhgu
will laugh when you cry sad
to make your world happy
Gugun gugun buree 'gukoore doongge'
Wake up little buree your
old gulung boome
all gnumgnin to
love mooroon gunggen ge
Oh little buree goonduhmu sing
goonduhmu the feelings of
gurring ina narmee, gurring ina narmee
nha gun goon na nhorn goo
yea little buree our binung love
your sounds in the boorun
now miremumbeh and
monu goondir helps
little black gukoore your gumee
loves you. Even mumu love you

Quick Sing (Translation)

I can see a lot of people coming
Little black baby
You must respect the moon
You must praise the sun
You must seek love with the star
Little black baby hear your
song: 'That's our country'
The willy wagtail
will bring the message
The kookaburra
will laugh when you cry sad
to make your world happy
Baby crying
Wake up little baby
old good catch
all me and you to
love a man singing out
Oh little baby sing
sing the feelings of
what am I doing in this flat country
I come from not here but long away
yea little baby our ear love
your sounds in the wind
now rain coming and
that clever doctor helps
little black kid your auntie
loves you. Even uncle love you.

Fellow Being

An' we aborigines in humanity.
The pulses of the red sun give a beat in aboriginal people.
The kissing of winds to trees are the love between aborigines.
Even the water we drink is the pure tears aboriginals share.
We wisely in our humanised aboriginal homes are united under
    all one colour.
The aboriginal is the bread of man's rich land.
We are the rocks of ages and purpling skies.
Look at every scenery in bush you will see an aboriginal face,
    body and spirit.
The aboriginal is not owned by any human being on earth.
Our presence is the flesh of fresh new worlds.
We are music that floats into a wonderful note to all ears.
An aboriginal is nature's soil, you pick it up, hold it in your
    hand and
you will feel our growth in the ground.
We are the gods of man in this land but then we are not
    humans.
Yet we are part of your kind now hey.
The earth above is our spirituals.
And now if you speak our tongue, don't mean you are native.
The sea, hills and lakes are in our hearts and minds.
The universe is belonga to dem big spirit creator.
Oh, now man you go out there to find out more of us, who
    down here.
Well listen to that fish talk and you will know we ate it the
    other day.
And if you talk to a bird of paradise you find they are people,
    same with
all creatures here, we aboriginals come from them.
If you feel the heat of the sun, you feel us.
If you see and feel the light of the darkness then you have just
    touched an aborigine.

Uppu Gulung Goowe
Good by and by

Aurukun oh Aurukun
Here we've heard
The cry of young people
Seeking love we will
all find Aurukun is
very much tribal
Aurukun near a sea
Aurukun beautiful land
We over or down here
must give spirits
Murri power, for you
our people
Aurukun as claps
even hidden things
But Aurukun is where
we fell in love
Aurukun to me down
this place hold my
heart in greater
respects for Kuoowta
firmly in looking after
our main mon
Aurukun where
is black power the
white church will
never give us the
related we to
understand your struggle
but let me say Aurukun
people now know this
hard world
But up the Aurukun Aborigine.

Am I

Am we lonely these days
Am I grief in the wind
Am us friend to nature
well hooked me up and
we'll fish
The dreamed dreams are
opened for wishes to come to life
Am you hurt
Am you to see me
We am and dem gonna
sleep and dreams of my people
There all alone in the mind
Murri stranger came to me
and said, Am I the one outside
you all getting spiritfully
When sun shines in the rains
we find summer here sooner
Treat my mother with a career
Treat conscience with rotten
education
Women are allowing bodies to
be taken
At last moment of life
Love even nobly came
against my skin
I heard a roo cry
Am I hearing attendants
to my hearts
Am we lovin' in these days
Am I sadden these nights
Forever it possess you man
something must tell
Am I me or you am us.

The Children

The children of not caring loveness,
and the losing loveness

Who loves their Father
loves their self
Who loves their dad
loves their sap
Who loves me I am the son
But who care for my
body unwanted
Who keeps my love
safe within
Your mum shines
dat hug around your world
Mixed emotions inner
your heart brings
all power to all
Yet this is not so when
Father has gone away
from mum's loves
who looks after us
now full is empty
love shares and cares
But who loves my dad and mum
Whose love love?

Consideration of Black Deaths (story)

'No treaty will give us our laws: it can be broken'
Two brothers were killed up here
didn't even have a chance to live
yes they lived short yet long
cos we never forget them
Two sisters up here are dead
by rape and knife cuts
They were drunk with white men
Yes it's not all their fault
yes don't blame the white-eyes
It's the societies dat the
rich pigs control.
The sheets and blankets of the cells
are a danger to us
The disposable razor are a danger to us.
Now correctional man in times
you have broken the law
how was it when you didn't know
our custom and cultures
you didn't know my tribe
my people's land needs
you didn't feel for us yet
you moved on me with a
untrue law and rules
Yes my correctional man
what happen to the brothers up at Rocky
did you know they were sad
and dat Lawton was sentenced on a white law
Now he was found hanging
from a sheet, now how come
the wired net was not
over the window hey correctional man?
You have ended him as a black man death over life
he needed in his family

Yes, I didn't know him face to face
but I felt his anger as a Murri
Like Robert Hopkins, it does all mean something
he was found wrist slashed and hanging too
yet he wrote to all who are proud to be abos
you hear his voice singing these words
'How many more blacks must die before the white man will
   understand'
To be back with the family in jail is hard.
Yet they know there is a way out of every ways.
Now in jail Murri men and women needs a black law
so they can come to live a better life and give more
to their community.
The royal commission will come and go I say,
but why is there still deaths of my people.
Well they sit and discuss here and there,
that's OK, yet why not support a more push
to get an aboriginal prison based on helping get good jobs
and culture working in the prisons.
The commission does a lot of good work,
yet it's in the custody of the same white lawless society
that oppresses us.
Yes go into the watch houses and find the evidence,
but remember the back hurt my Murri will feel when you
   leave.
J. Pilot may have been stopped,
by having a doctor on the job at the jail.
And dat young girl locked up in a cold room
will she be given a fair law to look into,
of why this happened.
I say aborigines are scared of evil spirits
dat white man and
women ways
so for a start you put us in there to rot
and rotten it is.

Yes we've broken your laws and this is wrong to you.
Well we are native people denied too long our rights
to a cultural law of our own.
We believe in the light of good
we are honest until we are found black death in custody.
210 years we are in the custody of white people.
Even our homes, land, sky and air your law hurt us
make us sad when we are glad
give us grog and we take it to the limit,
like punching up in a fight between ourselves
yes we do kill one another
yes we do undo our race,
but this is helped by your work in keeping white power alive.
I am like the wind too, we change.
But you have left my people in a unchangeable way.
They see it's fit to break and enter your white homes.
Roll your man for money, even some black men say to
   themselves,
let's rape this white woman for they are white with a past of sin.
Now I don't want my people to just hurt white people for the
   fun of it.
But do it in a school, educated speaking, writing rap, dat will
kill them with the truth, rape their minds
tell pure in Murri thinking.
leave their bodies for they undo themselves.
you Murri prisoner in there now
must fight with minds at ease
cool, calm, and knowing we care, love and think of you all.
First the representing of Murris must be Murris
get rid of migglou who are there
like this Premier Goss.
Not doing much for Murri culture, law and land rights
is a sell out brother
he is just a white man dressed to kill the real justice of all land
owned by black law
without the white law interfering.

20   NEW AND SELECTED POEMS

Now we have a black top man in this department of black affairs.
You see Murri, anyone goes and work for white controlled place
have to be coated paint of black but think white.
Now Les Melzer don't say overturn
you are just patronising our own people,
cos if you wanta do something, get all white out of there
and say this a Murri revolutionary takeover
but you Les are paid by white Ann Warner.
Get it Murri Prisoners
it's a fight everywhere.
Our people are more confused than ever.
You see, the prison you in is our prison
yet we have the opportunities
anyway let's get all Murri to stop this hanging
or trying it out of the life we need to build.
Like you I'm lonely too
I feel like killing himself too,
but I don't want some white law find me out of my mind or
    insane
I feel, think I will do myself in,
Yes, kill, die get out of this too,
for like my other brother and sister I must do it.
Where's the sheet and blankets and razor and anything else?
Then a sound came over my room
'Here it's nigger boy'
'Here it's abo boy'
It was the correctional officer and a police officer say
'Look he's drunk, mate lock him up with no mattress or
    blankets'.
Lucky I woke up, this was not a dream,
and thinking my bed it's the 1990s
and still my Murri die up here in QLD.
Well I'm off to see you soon
and tell you,
you're not to blame for what you've tried to take your life.

We all have attempted suicide since whites came to our homes.
We've hurt, cried and died.
Yet we have lived a life happy.
My Murri prison will be a prison of learning to get ways
of not returning to prison.
The dark love is not seen but I see you all.
The large wall I seen
but I have been through it.
My love for you as dying prisoner is living to free you
our fight for your cultural freedom is not over yet.
But I'm here not free to their law.
Yet free under the Murri law.
Sure we got to work out our Murri law, work alongside Murri
  law.
Yes dat must be done with you all
dead and alive even unborn
The prejudice is real in the schools
so it's real in the prison
The racisms are rebated and born
all the time with this country,
cos of the many people who
are dumb affair scared and uneducated

The stress is great in all Murri
family cos not enough talk action
of all Murri to our culture and
giving a way to fight the
love losted in years.
Yes many more is to be said
but one Murri will have a
mind broken down to the ground
if we say what really is happen.
But we must do it.
Self-determination is part of all
Murri family spirits. We will get
our heritage in the canoe

and sail on the beautiful life.
Yes prepare now man in jail
the time has come to your time
yet when you get out, it's back
to the same thing alcohol, drugs
and hurting each other. Yes, know
is hard to cool the lack of boredom
but you must try.
Our identity most us know
but do we arrest the ones dat
disobey the little you gave to life.
Brother you were out there
in front of the demo but what
did it give you freedom or to go
back in for more.
When one die in jail all of us die outside.
When one dies out here, you live to fight
so no-one die on the inside.
Yes commissioner you're white
The Murri prisoners are short in life
but long in spirits.

Rae Shines in Rivers

Little Rae of shine
Rae, your eyes shine upon your hair
Rae, in dreaming you shone
it happen a week ago July
my thinking of your closeness
towards my brother
Rae, a week seem long in love
Free spirits came over a
little ray of sun.
Free love must be given
if not then I'm lost forever.
Rae, the day we meet
is the day we kiss
Back there in dreaming
Back there in time
young and old, Murri as Murri
A little ray of sun shine
a little flower off the land
I ask this of a mind thing
I ask this of a love thing
Rae give me nothing
Rae I gave nothing
Rae I'm willing to give
Your kind voice I enjoyed
Your care I'm after
Rae you don't know me
Rae I don't know you
Trust must come of age
Livin' must come one day
But Rae my dream is a reality
But Rae my feeling is a happy one

Come sweet pretty Rae
Come on young in wiseness
Rae this was a dream of thinking
But will you understand a happy man?

Come Over Murri

I just remember Murris not only you die
in prisons or from poor conditions
Over other countries they're dying too and prisoned for
 surviving
like Latin America, where white man still tried to cause
 divisions with murder, rape and oppressions for exploitation.
We are not the only sufferers.
We are not just the ones fighting for land cultural rights.
Overseas in other lands they are fighting against the same
 enemy
which is capitalist or gone wrong commos.
We are in one world, but we here are forgetting about other
 native people's struggles.
We as Murri must look here and support the necessary
 struggles of other countries, for their fights affect our fights.
Take the black out of South Africa and put them here we will
 find the same racist things.
Take red people up in Canada, they're still fighting for rights.
Take the Pacific natives they are still struggling for what they
 need.
And take whites overseas, they are fighting too, oh, like the
 Irish people who want Britain out.
So Murris we have to have feeling, thinking and action for all
 low, small native peoples overseas.
And then we will get world understanding and unity, even love
 for one another's cultures.
Just remember they die, fight too Murri.
The other countries are waiting now for your support and fight.

Memo to Us (story)

Fortunately Australia has been given back to Aboriginals now.
   I'm sorry to tell you your passport is out of date, you must all leave this place. QLD is no more yours, white queen of England, it's been given to the natives. NSW has been deserted by the whites for some time now, the blacks have taken over. Tasmania is run by blacks who ran the devils out, and VIC is total abo control, so gubba have not got even a batman chance. SA is taken by forceful music singer blacks, and the whites are gone. They just didn't want a tribal law. WA blacks destroyed all modernised houses and put the poor together with the rich, over there no white power runs. The NT, has changed all faces, tongues to blackfella.
   Now here in Australia no white race lives, they are lost at sea and sent to spaces. So it took not long to restore all the natural things back to life. So it began to flower with new love, dreaming and sharing and care. The lands turn to paradise, beautiful rivers, hills, soil rose to greet the aboriginal race. Happy the days they hunted for food, greatly aboriginals respected each tribes. On forever, the land was filled and re-filled with behaviour of loving their own.
   Yes, this time the migglou made a mistake by giving us the land back. Then us, we aboriginals all garden for a ceremony.
   One tribe stood up proud and said, 'we are land, we have re-lived and we have beaten, killed the whites, but are we humans? We got to let them back to live.' Then out came a painted white man dancing a dance they did at pubs.
   Of course all the blackfellas clapped, saying and danced, 'til the dawn awoke with the sun showing the colouring of many a day so wonderful. The time came at the fire to eat the goanna, roos, fruitnuts and other things. Everyone was so full, they laid under the biggest tree for a rest before going home. At noon the aboriginals all thanked each other, then off they went in their peaceful surroundings. From the sea up above came a poor ghostly sound saying, 'I mean my race to do you abos no desecration, we are the white ones whose city roaring homes

are gone, but will you please, oh aborigines, let us back to live in harmony with youse.' All the abos said: 'look white race if, and dats a big IF, we let you back you must obey one rule, never be greedy. And anyhow, our new world is without the things you need, like wars. Oh migglous, go on, find your souls, that's what you gotta do.'

   At this time the poor old migglou ghostly sound faded into infinity. By now all Aboriginals were cooeeing cooee voices up and up so their spirits won't tire again. Now Australia is living in a heavenly camping home for all aboriginals. Of course, you whites out there are spaced pigs out into a time unknown. But us Aboriginals have the new stone age and science knowledge to bring you back to earth. Oh well, this part of land anyway. Immense and credible to your mind. But this one thing all abos think.

Yindingie Will Return Yenningee (story)

Once a group of Murri were cast adrift in a canoe sailing to a new land.

The waves were kind, the sun shone on them lightly and the night wasn't cold. The canoe carried towards the south where a young boy sung out, 'Land, land with trees and life.' Everyone was not afraid but eagerly waiting to get there so some jumped in an' swam to the shore. The sand felt good, so they yelled, 'We made it to the land of good spirits.' So after many moons they built gunyahs and created a tribe of all sharing. No-one looked sad, everyone ate food that gave them stronger bodies, and then one early morning the young boy who saw the land looked up to the sky to give thanks to their God. When a plane flew over the land and then back over dropping a big box wooden. Everyone ran to look at what was in it, cos it broke on the fall down. An old man said, 'This is not a good sign, look it ticks.' Then around it a dance was made. Up and down, around everyone danced. Then the plane came back over again and a voice loud saying, 'You must leave, this is not your land, die if you stay.' So the Murri looked at the canoe and all said now we don't know what this creature wants. Then in the afternoon the plane came and loud sounds yelled, 'Die blackie, die.' Of course the Murris were ready with a spear, they found like a rocket and blasted the plane out of the sky. And then looked at the box and it spoke out loud, 'Y'have destroyed the plane, now help me out of this box.'

So the Murri men lifted the big thing out. It was a battery run TV and was on. So all the Murris watched it for days and nights until it showed a true killing of a native race that looked like them, and spoke like them. Up jumped the young boy and threw a rock and smashed the TV in half. So they made a fire big enough for all the world to see, and everyone jumped into the smoke and went up to the sky god.

Who said to them: 'this is for your home, not down there. It will be ended by me sooner or later.' The young boy said, 'but father, where did those things come from?'

'Well boy, that is what you might say a bad race of people who want to control all the world with robots and machines. They are destroying themselves. So you are safe here by my fire water land and the universe is waiting for you to make a family. Just forget about them who are evil, bad, for we are to live in spirits. Come back to earth the day the goodness will prevail and love rules in control. 'The explorers of earth are losing tons cos they can't figure out what make them go round or breathe air, even die there. Yes, my Murris, you will never cast adrift anywhere and be bound with insane men. I am Ngunda Biral even Biamie they call me. I am greater than them cos I don't lie. So young boy, grow with the power so you may return with the message of me to all. I will call you a powerful name Yindingie, my speaker, singer, dancer.

   'Now go look after your people.'

Sue and Du
The spirit of one tribe is all

The Wakka Wakka are there
walking, talking singing
in the land.
The Gabi Gabi are there, walking
talking, singing in the land.
The Gurang Gurang are there walking,
talking, singing in the land.
The Dungidau are there walking,
talking, singing in the land.
The Booyooburra are there walking,
talking, singing in the land.
They are all full blooded past and
futures. They are looking at us
doing what's wrong — yes they are
listening to us, saying silly things
Do you remember dat story
No it was never told. Yes
but can you sit in the bush and
think of the chants peace they had.
Can you sit and easy your spirit
to feel their presence
can your mind picture what
they looked painted up like.
Yea Murri it's hard when few
are here, but some have
spoken long time ago, some are
here today willing to tell us.
Have you ever heard of Fred Embrey?
Well his stories are recorded in
book, may be taped. And have you
heard Willie Mackenzie — he gave
knowledge to migglou of lot of
tribes many old are still here
walking, talking, singing. Where
are they dat come from the land?

You Murri of today have it here
speaking, telling and reliving.
Wakka, Kabi are still there
they are all there in the wind,
rain, sun, bush morning and night;
you will feel proud to be Aboriginal
if you give all your tribes
the POWER TO LIVE.

I'm Not Santa

Black santa is sad cos he found he's sacked
The Christmas has come again
messing up the family's saving
The kids at school sing praises
of a silent holy night and a
tree to be cut down for presents
And they wait for the big red
bearded white santa man to
come down the chimney
And they think this is true
but the jingle media suck dem
in to buy everything at high price.
And what the black parent
say to their childrens is, who
the bloody hell is christ coming
here and stealing our culture
with deer and sledges?
Then you all turn and sing
merry christmas, well this
is a profit making business
for the rich, don't you know childs?
Christmas destroy the poor
and it's a fake unto happiness
Christmas is against the Murri
belief cos it celebrate one man
birth and not all men.
Sure you'll get me to a black santa
but remember I'm just cringe
inside cos you're too young
to explain the political cultural
sad oppressed nature this so-called
xmas caused to our people before.
And even right here, the image of
santa forgets neglects the poor dark
childrens even white kids, why?
cos santa is the capitalist who's there to

fool you and drain your dad and mum of
every money they have.
Now how can you be merry when your
cuz relative got nothing or people starving or
people live in bad homes.
How can you merry on
a day when the world is at war for peace.
Well if in your heart you want to be merry then do it every
moon, full star shine and dawn morning
And catch the sun up before SANTA comes and
takes your PRESENTS!

Frisky Poem and Risky

Regarding respects I'm fully
purchased within my own
exchanges
Please give my regards to our
God down and above
I would also like more spirits
so the list can be send
Before receiving your hearing
I had to write to a conference
Sincerely I'm yours against
all evil co-ordinators
I decided from myself stems
a meaning and a creation
The prices I payed in every
eye ear and tongue will
wish they gave the correct addresses
My project have been pulsed
by blacks, and repriced
rejected too personally politically
This document I place, will be
the birth shown
A division by me is true
of knowledge in poetry
I've got history information
My date rave into sane real
I am amended then lended
Are you prepared for the
Nee Nee who died
I anticipated my pissed mind
I wish to withdraw all
my poems from the
building and put in the
open spaces.
As for gardens of me growing
out to another country
I may do honestly

My heart ain't pure love
My brain ain't poison daze
Ngunda Bimiai spoke the message.
All I did was draw this.
All I did was pass on
But one thing they gave me
is my own selfing self.

Just Woke Up

I am waiting for friends to come and the Bus came.
I have immense silence here in my land
I watch SBS and ABC if there's anything on blacks.
I go walking up the gulleys of white properties
When we find a spot to sit and fish, white man says
move on.
I have ten acres of just dirt no flower, plants, trees,
a cow donkey and one migglou horses . . . koalas roos
passing by.
Five dogs one duck and I'm gonna get more with my
next cheque
I put our blackfella flag up high in a tree out front,
but migglou came and took it down
I am alone but surrounded with peoples in the
skies clouded.
Happiness rest in the fires I make out back.
I worry dat yesterday I didn't write a poem for them
Murris. And I hear today a Uncle is coming to teach
the jarjums more corroboree, but this uncle is a
believer of jesus bible thing from jews
So I don't know how to sing dance dat old black
magic cultures.
I just have a drink and smoke and if clean up not
done the swearing wife come out yelling or throwing
hints. I was born in another tribal country but
I'm living here with the love spirits of this disappeared
tribe.
Here I am immense in silence yet I'm still wilder in
mind I am your writer FRIEND.

Poem in Binga to You

I love her she as her fretters of live but I have hurt her maybe me hurt me but will make her HAPPY. She is having a day of joy happy thirtieth years of celebrations. Her body has grown, her mind has riped and the maturity of her soul is like flying to a nest of life. She dislikes her father's moods when he brings bad past things to her family, and hate it when he hits and swears at her mother.

She's sadness in her eyes for him and prays he change before she is old. She feels he don't speak the right manner at home but she loves him at times of happy moments. She carries the tune in her mother's words and feels deep in her care, even learns things from her dat she needs to combat the evils of some living. She thinks in her mother's mind but develops her own thoughts. Cos she loves her not just she born her yet for her mother quiets sleeps and cook clean in the camp of Jagera for her. She respects her in full Murri spirits. Well the day's come and the sun will shine for she knows this the day she must be happy forever and causers of the bad in man. Her name is part of the moon and even the emus has place in her life. She clearly proud of herself and loves her bros and sisters. She is not a woman but has fought like one and now her cake will be eaten and Ngunda her god will bless her heart and soul forever. She has a home and tribe of both parent and she believes in music to listen and play. One thing is she is Murri and ready to fight her father if necessary to defend her mother's family. She is Moocoo, a thirtieth emu.

Weather Comes

The weather is wearily
The winds are webbing
blowing voices of help
Sun is lowering its light
moon is darking its face
stars is fallen its flight
rain has rained non stop
sea waters raised higher
rivers swallower and
banks fall apart.
Trees grow old no more
Fruits grow wilder no more
Raw uncleaned smelling
air goes in the plants soils.
Ochres shows colours unseen.
Sand dirt mud soot all look
different, touch different,
smell funny.
We can't hardly believe this
was once our dreamtime home
The sky turns strangler and
clouds hide behind smoked
pollutions.
Pollutions walking the bush
slips feet unfound, and seeks
sound unheard. Sleeping
never rests in our human
minds, for fear terror follows
about day and night.
The weather is a changed by
man's interfering
Our respects for seasons for
hunting and gathering is
untogether mixed up. Feelings of
heat rushes sweat all over bodies
hurting
Feelings of cold shivers blood
veins frozen.
The weather is changed.

She Sang

We are like tunes sung out of songs
We are hostile dat brings life and colour

To cling to customs To uphold our rights
you and I come to dance
We are like birth be born in a dream
Yes imagination and change are with you
today.
At night the sun came bright
At morning the sight you saw no light
Yet our eyes shone lights all of the land
in shame
We are many several hundred faces
Yet we can't properly see your face
around this place
Some had ears in tune with birds
sing in the dawn
Yet when children ran to hear and see
none was there, just a old woman singing
a song: 'We are like tunes
             yet you are to lose
             MMM I'm yours told by law
             We are to tune to be true
             Come child, come child
             Back to love life, a lovie
             We are like tunes.'
The childrens stopped listened and looked and
became joyful cos the sound gave them
sight feel touch and love.
Then a shadow sweeped over the area,
it was large with no wind
Looking up everyone saw dark woman
sitting on a cloud singing in Murri.
             'Stay where you are jarjum
             Stay and it will be alright
             Your land is caring and you
             will share in it. She spirit
             of love will keep you strong.
             So Bye Bye mother nature
             will return.'

Farewell Reverberated Vault of Detentions

Today up home my people are
indeedly beautifully smiling
for the devil's sweeten words are
gone.
Today my people are quenching
the waters of rivers without grog
Today my people are eating delicious
rare food of long ago.
Tonight a fire is made round
for a dance of leisuring enjoyment
where no violence fights stirs.
Certainly my people are god given
a birthright of wise men and women
Our country is still our Motherland
Our desires ain't dying in pitifully
lusting over contempt and condition
Tonight my peoples sleep
without a tang of fear
No paralysed minds
No numbed bodies
No pierced hearts hurt
The screams of madness ends
The madly stretched endurance
are resisted with Murri faith
The enchantingly lonely
pains by white constipations
are pushed gaped nailed by
our emerging loves for
primitive's potentials.
Tonight overturned hells
brang surface innocent olds
Tonight my people don't wait
for successions of society
But yell, sing the souls to
our endless dreaming

Today my people have a Murri
Thirtieth century culture
but with care safe and snarls
Today my people feel precious as
human beings burials and birth
Mankind demands imperative love
for all, And my people never
wants to escalating barbarous century.
For now Today up home they free,
Tonight they learn to fight consciences.

Little Murri
Be a Murri before an Australian

Little Murri boy you just coming forward
Little Murri boy be happy at the school
It's all you got for a while.
Little Murri boy be glad you not
livin' in the 1950s or 1970s 80s
Little Murri boy I hear you say
I'm proud to be an aborigine
Little Murri boy we know you
have a migglou mate who is proud
to be an Australian
Well little Murri boy give the
love of your culture to all
But never let dem buy your spirit
never let dem sell your sensitive land
For you little Murri are
one to unite the lost white childs of Australia
Little Murri boy come back to
the grave of your people with
respects to clean the bad tales
Little Murri boy always give love to
your mother and father.
Little Murri one day you will
grow and realise dat your school
is in travelling your country
and getting rich off honesty
faith and making the right
decisions
in life.
Little Murri boy you will fight
physically among other, well just stake it out one step at a time
They say words are tougher than a bullet

You dig young Murri boy
be cool straight and work
Be a worker not a writer
Be a singer not a digger
Little Murri boy shut out hate
shut out black racism and cut out white racism.
Little Murri boy, I'm the voice of the mission years
yet you little Murri boy holds
my and our country in your brain.

For Garney (Garnet Fogarty, L.F.'s grandson)

Drunk Cricket Field No. 1

Roy stands so tall dark, not out for a duck
Glances, side cuts at a bad pace
Roy he's our cricket player
Laying the grounds with tactics
Smiley Hands are swift fast and to the
catch without a drop
His team's males are top batsmen even bowlers.
Under the guides of a good eye
Roy bowls up a blow
tin slump stick slump fall
at this Murri-man Border
Roy Weazel
'Weazels' those even
better throwers.
Yet he can spin it up and
tests the wind with fingers.
Roy you will never see him
in a drunken real cricket mood.
Smiley, we look at you taking
up what great Eddie Gilbert done.
Barambah cricketers are in sensational
matches surrounding fields.
Dat wickets and batsman on the other side
will lose under Roy's coaching.
The runs are up, the big score is coming
Roy had series played everywhere in Qld
Obstacles at first ball dashes past
this cut shot innings player
83 runs and he must be a winner an' giver
Their bails are whipped off and
Roy got run out, then more young
Came just to appeal at the umpire
Roy is the person who knows about cricketers
be it the pad on your legs or the mask they wear
Roy might toss beer and wine for this time
But he feels greater than those Bradmans

Mr Weazel walks sways runs like a
genuine captain.
You may not say so, yet look at our brother's
'over arms' 'under arms' body moves.
You and the black and whites games win or lost
make us wanta jump shout up with sheerer
victories. Smiley comes across a boosted supporter too
No bowlers gonna get more overs nor catchers hiss hiss
on me blood relation Smiley Weazel.
Roy get a wild, but keeps his cool grounds
He's terrific. Tops and must be self-educated
in historic cricket.
Roy's Mulla doses in pain after game
The bat is his life, the famous cricket
have to take notice of his advice
Roy to me in first class match
But unpaid in this spot match
Englishmen Roy knows we been mates
stick cricketing lovers your years.
Last season Roy get dem gut
Hat tricks awaits your smile
Those up coming darkie will remember
Your keenness and ways you
thrash an attack with ruthless
hard-hitting right-hander rash stroke
Roy the honours is yours even when they barrel
You a leg spin bowling
go out you're stumped 'Buda'-budda
Roy drunken brilliant cricket teller
Give dem a gaping hole, wickets won't stand.
Roy stands so tall dark not out for a duck, Ha
Medium pacers will cop it from Roy
Superb team mates aligns in talents skills
Roy's task will snared many deliveries
Confidence shows on your face at a game
Cos you promote dat high lights of an innings

Roy grand final struck forward
and your unbeaten record will be remembered
Roy Weazel particularly strong when
driving a delivery.
With a classy cricketers Roy ensues
he'll first toss and elect
Roy stuck a chase indoors and outer
Roy progresses mind fully towards grades
whose get caught mid-off off
You have the knack and the wack wacka
Roy is a match winning for his people
Gloves wearin' on his hand, hat over his head
Now Roy's ready for nine hundred maidens
Aww Roy is sharp and steady at a swing
The compliments go to you R.T.M.W.
Ya bloody drunken black reliable cricket star
Come on Roy don't fit just get dem fitter.
10:00 p.m

Where Have You Been

A-where have you been gone
A-where have you been, where have you been gone
With my Murri love
A-where have you been to go with my Murri love
You come from a time before
You come from a time forward
We know our land lame and tame
We say the land about now
But where are you my Murri love?
But where are you my Murri love?
Hardened by the rain, hardened by the day
Saw the sun, I work for the sun
I saw a graveyard undertaking by a man's ways
We know our land are same
We know you are the Murri man
Come, what did you see?
Well I've seen you love lost
I've seen you lost, I've seen time sitting under the streams
That love you want will come
That love you want will come
But you will fight blazing a-blazing
In a Murri peace man
Murri love, oh where have you been, my Murri love?
Back to back you are black
Forward to forward you are black
You come from time that will give us our time
I met you once before
I met you once in a forward dreamtime in our future

Surviving Dreaming Surviving
on Biame Dreaming, by Garnet Mickelo

Biame creator — Supreme Mythical Legend
creators of Aboriginal Murri Dreamings
Journeys I've traversed — strengthened
Ngrandra unified People Law
Unforgotten Trials, travels must journey
Through lifes treacherous most walks
within Aboriginal Murri Dreamings
People and Land IS Law — sustaining
Aboriginal and Rain is My protein
Rain and Water and Fire and Rain
Sweetness of being spirited truly — LIFE
How old is that tree . . . ?
Where do those rivers run . . . ?
Rainbow Rain Reflections — Is it?
Whatever is omitted actively spirited
Is inflicted, same reflective response
Love and Respect respectively — ever
Pridefulness, journeys I've travelled
Biame creator — Supreme Myrthical Legend
Existence of Aboriginal Murri — Dreamings
Journeys just begun, I've traversed
        PEOPLE AND LAND IS LAW
Earth and Wind and Fire and Rain
Unforgotten, trials, travels, must journey
Strengthened . . .

From *Jagera*

Rocko Langton

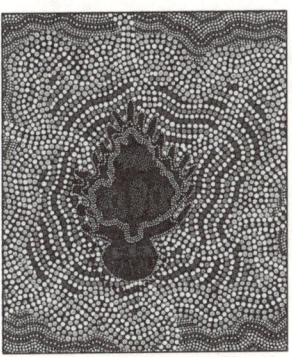
Garnet Mickelo

Charles Chambers

1990

Love

Love . . . walk with me
Love . . . waken with me
Love . . . is a black newborn
Camp fringe dwellers are my love
Love is not seen in cities
Love is my Father
Love is my Mother
Scrubs are hid in bush love
and we say
Love's mine.
Love is alive and received.
Love is a kangaroo
Love is an emu
Love is the earth
Love is the love of voice
Love is my friend.
And what about us
who has no love?
Well, love smells.
Us Murris knows
It's love in bad love.
Give us love. Give us love.
Our Dreamtiming is love.
Catch my love over a fire
Fire of love.
Culture is our love.
Culture is ourself in love.
The school don't give love
so we black power give you love
Proud and simply
love is the love
to our lands love.
Love walk with me
Love awaken with me
Now give us the true love.

Mad Souls

I am a moody Murri
my temper as black as me.
I am a moody Murri
drink and smoke,
sail me away to Africa.
Yes, I'm a moody Murri
I live to swear
and shit anywhere.
I am the moody Murri
don't like Aussies
don't like Asians.
You'd love to meet me.
I'll tell you
go live where you come from.
I am the Murri black
here forever.
Sometimes can't stand my own people
some sell out
some sell off.
I am the blackfella you need
in governments.
If I am asked about, pay the rent
I'll give it a go mate.
I am the moody blue Murri.
Please don't take offence
your own negative reply.
I am not mad
but glad.
Roots grown out
Mingling with shining desire
Free our dreams
Yet you people miss what I am
and
I am the moody Murri
My temper as black as me.

Boundless Guides

Mocked as nothing off shore
Them possess a grief
Moreton Bay banished our native shore
More adore those settlements in chains
More mining sands, condemn our lands
Moreton Bay belongs to painted clay people
More underneath ambush monsters
are bewailing for our natives
to keep treating.
Them blacks got mangled, flogged
feeling the lacerated back.
Our mythologies are ours owned
by dreams unstained
was they to know creation to fall . . .
Here Moreton as we aspire your Island
We last strong winged sails
From shore epics anew to white
from white mens crew.
It's a warm sea cries, that's in your eyes
If a bright merry spring winter or love
reach out you Bay Murri
We miss our way of living
Bay to banks attained in your noon
Morning dew quarrel a people
over Moreton Island.
And mans darkest progression
are poisoning your unawakened sense.
A coloured dreaded recoil migglou
are nameless, your home Island.
These Moreton blackfella
lower our history
flacked to fade.
Come back hearts, beginning a beat
Making believe in willing native
affectionate towards clearer washed sky
even white people must leave this place.
Don't Moreton Aborigines rush in spirits
of an onward sunlight.
Suddenly these days, their people
come to mind.
No enemy by black.

FROM *JAGERA*

For I Come — Death in Custody

I
in a jail.
Even a Murri wouldn't know
if him free.
The land is not free.
Dreamtime is not free.
No money needed.
See that scarred hand at work
that's cutting away
to freedom
Freedom.
Jail not for me
but a lot of my people in jail
White jail are cruel
Set up the family, stay away
come to see your Murri
look big and grown
in learning, of our gods teaching.
What they give you in here?
Away from the corroboree
In the fuckin' jails
Murri get out, so we can fight
like the red man has done
Lord them a come.
My brother die there
in white custody
And I hate the way the screws patch up
and cover up.
He died at the white hands
it was there, in the stinkin' jails
up you might blacks
Him not free
For when white man came
it's been like a jail
with a wife and a family
black man can stay in jail
like it's home.
Fuck, they hung us all.

For brother D.L.

For Aussie Mates of Natives

He is a white brother and he drinks
relate at a Murri feelin'
He is a white yubba
has a dog and cat
T.V. and food, lot sometimes
white yubba got music
Yea, him got no wife
Yea, him got big family
They call Australians
He's a white brother
he saw the city people
all living with wars in minds
Yet he learn this from only Murri people
Yea, he's my yubba, be it white
He pays the rent
Yea, this is the day we get what's ours
Yo, white brother has helped
in little ways
But he's our white yubba
even dances with us
sings with us
Yillul yillul to this white mate
Mmmmm . . . he's my yubba
his eyes are different
yet he's a friend of friend
relates to me as human being
then there's no race or colour
La la, him my mob mob
Oh, didn't see you there brother mate
wake up now
my Murri mates ain't white
So here's to the white yubba
bring me to the end
This is all Murri have
for white yubba . . .

For Andrew

Ngunda ... The God

J.C. is not true. 'Is this true?'
Ngunda is true
For the Murri, it's time to change
Give us the black god
who fights physical
and spiritual
Let them come at sea
Let them come to tame
J.C. is not true
believe me Ngunda is real
speaks to your updated mind
in Dreamtime
Yea, what is your God
Our's been different name but same creator
Tell them lost, drunk Murri
it's time to rhyme
Ngunda is an Aboriginal
God shared every soul
You have a band
You have a land
and J.C. don't come from this Nulli Wo land
Just made it to Ngunda, Biami religion
We are a lot of blacks, with the same culture
working together.
Be you live, long way there
we still here with Ngunda.
Come take sorcery feeling away
Is Jesus Christ true
Blackfella, well he's from Ngunda world.

Kath Walker

We are coming, even going
I was born in 1957
the year after I became a realist
I am a full blooded black Aussie
we want racialism
you got ostracism
black ascendance
Charter of Rights, she said
Hey, now they got dependents
exploitation is being done here
Self-reliance, not compliance
most will say, resign
circumscribe the enemy, not befriend
they will give oversight and
human segregationary rights.
No choice. No colour conscious.
Give us bigots who are not biased
Give us prevention, not ambition
Status, not condescension.
Give us Lord Christ and confidence
all we do is fellowship bureaucratic protection.
Give me settlements, camped in missions
Prohibition
from old, young time.
Thank you. Education makes us equals
Opportunities are disheartening
we defend white over-lordship
rebuff the independence
my laws ain't no cold choice.
Native, old salvation seller
we are the conquerors to take over
not Christ
So our land in law
must rank out aliens
in our banished race
though you baptised by
Just black . . .

Bungoo Bungoo

Models are not derived from books
Now this is untrue, got nowhere to go.
Give me money, so incidents may
come to life.
I will masquerade as a poetic
deep and abiding in black oppression.
Give me money, so I can travel over this
Give us money so we can see and hear.
Our Aboriginal human race
want bungoo . . .
Utilised how can I write
staying one place, at home
knowing I write for Australians
native and white.
Give me money for my worksminds
Priced on lives
and dressed in peace
You will rip my justice apart
Con your promises
Brings us nothing.
When crippling writer write
you look to jump over them, hey
Poet haters told to shut us up
Poet, me lovers told to shut up
Me so low in money.
No we are forced into dumps
where money are nations.
Nations are turned to face
money.
But our struggle will bring life.
Help me rich
or give money
you money faced opposition.
I just want more to give more . . .
He is deprived of money

Will you give some paper junga
to help a poor father
with seven children
at home
writing about you and his people
Thanks for nulla, nulla . . .
Meaning in this is money.
Junga.

'Dulpai — Ila Ngari Kim Mo-Man'

Moppy, Aborigine, Gumbal Gumbal was he
Aborigines King Billy was him; lived
loved him people
around Tampa lands.
Lowood ancient copper blacks
never alive in them town camps.
Nature shared our environments
with physical effects
men, black was aware of that bush secret.
Then interwoven, fictional settlers
came upon their homes.
Tents went up. Gunga. Mia-mia.
Burned away. Torn, blown
Taken tribal implements, damaged.
Warlike colonies half-hearted
a magnificent death
on honest young Aborigines.
Race at Kilcoy, a bloody massacre.
Peace to a flower
gave more feeding to fires
of our escaping leaders.
High-pitched wails echoed
among a reddish-brown caraboo
named the great 'MOPPY'
Low voice, yet spoken aloud.
Ten clans, sounds confident
to your old fight
for even 1995 in future, lied Moy
boy and man will laugh mockingly.
Surprise them at morning rise
make useful every member of our tribe

Moppy
Our ceremonies made sure that the children's
tribal nation, would and will
grow to prosper.

Dared, afraid, trembled.
Mr Moy Moy thought to make you
their prey after dark.
Moppy went to his people
gleaming eyes ready
to cold ray an evil whispered violent
flickering sign.
Moppy declared defiantly:
Elders we noisily here a startled voice
crashing solidly through this
civilised families drifted apart.
These were and are wrong, almost impossible
furious revenge came over the muttering.
Moppy 'savage', claimed a white woman.
Well about this forgetting time
meeting sat at ground level
and Aborigines talked
how to avoid directly these horse, cattle people
who stay:

Moppy stood on a rock
and finished his speaking in front of
over 600 Murri blackies.
Kind Billy Tampa, let his axes be taken
and they antagonise him
visible, plain, quickly people of this day
and age, are guilty
cos them hold opposite direction
in-out our history.
Angry Moppy must and still du du in safety
confided in all Murri here
So we stood, walked, corroboreed, war
painted in honour
to divert awful living at present '90.

Moppy, my Aborigines sang happy
and gladly
at Moppy's swift actions.
Lead us . . . lead us . . .
Even with your magical spells.
We all strict to your commandments.
Except, except the empty stomachs.
of the boasted, with the loud voices
and waka, no support.
Previous fighter Moppy.
I'm yours,
young, even old, to follow:

Over previous 500 years we might turn back
our times, forward times.
Moppy, Moppy . . . poets wise we am?
Don't balk balk the hero. Inda
Youdu, you you build our cultures.

Looking up at Moppy's reflection, father.
Moppy thundered myself to repeat a clearer respect
irrespective . . .
The great strengthened Pemolroy pride
longer Murri calls, in feelings our same
'no shame'.
He show our world he cared
He's ancient, dilli blames the pain
Seize our brothers lame
Gross injustices, victimised miss the richer
and in waiting together
he futures a good education
pleasant for us Aborigines.
Tell it like it is
It's us who's on south laws
them are shadows to lifeless burries:

Up here blatant accidents
are made
to hand out lost wealth.
Now Mr Pemolroy
Australians scared us to death
not to fight.
Now control forefathers washed fears
We have no fear
we are clean
are we to inflame our truth:
My people over Australia . . .
Perth, Darwin, Cairns, Bamaga, Broken Bay Cove
and Port Phillip Bay
over Murray Bridge and into Oodnadatta . . .
Your Aborigines are not forbidden to think quickly
of your citizens.
Since trade arrival, they herded us
natives in thought, movements
so we think as them
and listen like systems of
controversy:

Well Moppy, Yagan, had respect.
Has private spiritual properties
If had learn a school option
Aborigines will find many Aussies
are 'dogs' within a potential 'dobbers' class
Governed like it was right
in your own neighbourhood.
Australia tribespeople are messengers
to arrange the visits
once on exchange
Our battle of sick men intruding
on small children's sounds, are mentally
wanderous
to hurt their camp feast.

Between Aborigines borders your ordeal
in screaming, robbing, discussing difficult
worked by a frenzy barrage of angry killing
of our beliefs.
When will eager poor fights erupt
our lightning bolts to the nam, Moppy
Furtively buried greeting threats:

Why waste the clenching fists
wild, sisters, flare a white insult
at last tempers striving companions
desperate clouds dust wattle
over and around those combatants
choking, fought insults
Moppy, Johnny Campbell . . .
Kagariu.
Clash of waddies or spears are helpless
to obscure,
this gashed groaning lost male.
Who have the half-dazed blacks roaming bush.
Now Aborigines only commence assault
cos those evil white or half whites
scratch and lash their minds
unbelieving
belief relaxing in homes:

Disobeyed.
The gods are what picked faith
will not hideaway.
In the next few moons
carried by our happiest challenge
love, are we willing to toughen coolamen.
Then a blurted shudder one gita morning.
Said Dundalli, attack
all through that long summer
so stagger their skilled mistakes.

So here are those instinctive moves
in migrant picking on an Aboriginal family.
And instead meat by mighty hunter
full-grown tricks me, your people
have to face:

   Unusually they crawled near their rich houses
asking beard or smoke — waterfire strangely
was curiously given.
That's true. When any black man goes to their fence
openly, wanting to speak face to face
to indifference that's been dropped . . .
them hide
their doubters sweetest decisions
just so they won't give up stolen love.
And our leaders will sing out
them is frightened of humans
one full to hear out.
This is the protest, not rested even
not honest, given of friendship
these days and nights
Oh great fighters in our region
to reach, jump on them from behind, cos trouble
are always overseas.
Forces sneak ageless, called careless
are what gubba man caution.
Wanta beware, for guns we can use
Not just whispered words:

   And some may chuckle
But we blackfella recognise them
at probably aroused times
timid, taught to live assailants.
Fire-blackened Lionel
I regained my senses
to secret the Murri world.
Submissively them shout terrible injustice
Where's the justice?

Duramula came to change
unbeliever to Aborigines present life.
Duramula is the voice bringer
Rhythm sticks we may hit
Rhythming a wavering power
won't give death
to those who have betrayed our leaders:

Changer of life
Punjel can change, boy into man
girl into woman
Boomed out an answer
now old women, louder and deeper
in the reality world.
Call them from their homes
And when they hear my voice
they must obey . . . Ngunda . . .
Me . . . Nulli . . . me . . .
Sender, bring him back to life
as they must return to camp
Singer you are now living.
Emerging my tribe once more
Clinging to my brother-mate
at homeland, Jagera
Moppy . . .
Wintu . . .
Gifted I am from Punjel, Duramula
While there is a sun married to the moon
We are to give a raised initiation
Tell Moppy and Lionel, poet Fo
Are them sell-out to express emotions unveiled
Punjel, mina lo run Da
Biamie.
For everything that You have given to me
I in return give back to you
Moppy.

From *Ngutji*

Rocko Langton

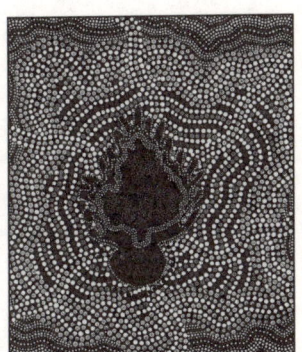
Garnet Mickelo

Charles Chambers

1984

The Buzz

City babes that now, were we moot moot
When he came nyarndi up
him sweet Koori
still, noondang him got jambi
boodoo between legs resting
heavily nya to camp late
at her calling
Binjou Binjou I am
Poor rich buildering
Goongal Goongal
Yeah moonoo moom same
have inter-understanding
take it brother, did you have a snort
aw cooni goona, buzzing on
you beena lied again
gubba sell this shit
We speak nya nya, nah
Koori his bro's to you
Bingoing and looking for good joonoo
In your moonoo
come on babes this snort
snort is mirigarn
you.
Ha, get up and see the brother
fight now for his judija
help you to know we is sacred
people takin'
My friend is cooni
My mates is rooted on
dirty dirty words
Like me only know this way
So babes, don't old
don't moot doori we.

Fuck All Departments

I takin' our comparative mis-saying
Down south of the law blacks roam
The dialect is harder to vocab
if you don't know.
Up south laws and the Dep. Abo Affairs
were like here.
Pick stealing our Koori Murri brains
where you sit, fire warmth
are you to set fire to buildings
so white, so right.
The Housing Co-op worker was fielding
in areas of gubba mentality
by making us pay rent on black own land
they say our Ha. Ha.
The bastards just like gubba
You can't give blackfella house
when him break, smash windows
walls, rip floors. Knock fences
down for wood.
For fire is our saving
electric bills . . . ha. ha. you black
Thinkin' migglou
Community controls means you don't
go National meeting swearing
declare war on governments
just your ways.
Everybody differ level
understanding family wantin' own
Ship was and is here now, this year
The money have to be spent by
the already set-up community operating
I'm staying in Department for a while
Well go fucken live in Canberra
Big money . . . junga you after hey?
Binna hearing conditions drawn by the gubba
pass down to you clowns
But been going around
This Jacky Jacky surrounded
Poor poor Koori

who getta caught
You come.
I yell hate, if let this community
go out of balance.
Get out of this gubba affairs
Ours await no more
We must fight you cunts too . . .
Truly open the public eye
open the party public servants
to black intervention
so we can clear you all out.
Again forces voiced by young people
must come out of age fully
Just better watch Koori persons
You smoking drinking don't speak
I'm into my community units
Us gotta concept of man
organised ability
Aboriginality is a very powerful
knowledge
of us . . . Ha . . . Ha . . .
All the best for Koori family
single you must feel
Department blacks you word-play
too much
a Koori term you selling south
Abuse us even when you office desk
push pens to get rid of us.
Justice shines with we people
Cos fightin' to fuck up
Dep. Abo airing saying
'I'm doing my best for my people'
jumper outer place when we pinpoint you
Telling truth. Them shit themself
Maybe we intimate your meeting
for our sake.
Light the burri.
Hear our Koori law.
Departments we destroy.

Love or Human Nature

Love originator is her Koori love's
Glad nearly complete with you
when not sad
possess we personally for the peoples
spirit and goal
bring me to Koori cause cos cos
Equally we like to be near bodys
Mother is woman
Nature are from Koori scoreness
respectfully comforts me here
Mankind . . . womankind . . .
even when man hypocrites
and black baits at the coloured bar
So love originator thousand
Stir in seen godfully gentle
to her black man now.
Or violent massing greedy boy or girl
will sway
late coming to home
a voice strong aware you
'take relevance and articulate
give strength, pride of a Koori language
Share your woman brother . . .
Nah . . . nah . . . don't live thata now downing.
The five paces behind . . . now . . .
up front expression desire
desire your own love
original womens.
I'm Murri Koori aboriginal
loving fresh and bold
see ya, told ya
us humanity
not discovered.
Gladly came
emerging just to our people
making love love love.

Ngunda Man Koori

When I'm taking you, it magic magic happy
As we drove across the waters
I said 'good fishing there'
Nah nothing there, they buggered
these waters up, brother.
Yea I can't relive this spirit
knowing I'll be there ... THERE.
The day went before the invasion to me
jumping out on to the Koori lands
bus, planes or trains
How come you feel this
Bro's you pulling my head
or bullshitting me, hey
Well Ngunda man
I am still in our land
As we felt tired, you let me
have bed and shower
Healing the patients
the societies nobody cares about me
Drunken blackfella
crying of a day gone by
and then, buy buy more nyarndi
Nyarndi. It may be better off
But I can't take to it
gives me a headache
dat cos you heading in the wrong heads
a Koori sang to me.
Red wine is dead dead
brother, to some winded
breathe women tidda drink
in beer wise speak
you just watch out tomorrow
gonna punch inta ya
Went to the tap in the 'Gents'
Drank sunk germs over red lips still.
Before you all get wild
All I was asking was where's the best place
to camp
Dial phones didn't work at my
see thing believer

FROM *NGUTJI*

Ha. I'm Koori
within light, even T.V. rooms.
We are what we are ...
we write about now
The struggle long wide dried passages
of unity
comes to me refighting
I don't wanta keep invading your mind
too easy ...
Don't blame me
thank yourself for being
outer gubba life
We rules are from a core
going inside lotta black feelin' too
My people drove me up to seasons
telling me to do this story
dreams reality for we
Oh. oh. spiritually there within
Koori dignity self respect
high flier me unto you.
Jubilee not for me to celebrate
in their white ceremonies minds.
Amazed wondering unheard
discriminating came over the lie
stars they waste
Heart blessed upturned you
When I said Ngunda man
is Koori earth ... wonderful.
Yea sisters and brothers
borning you now
now wait til how dumbfounded
me was or is.
Please surprise on my believing words
even tho ... even tho ...
I'm driving down to see you soon
The day by days rushes halo
heaven ... nah ...
Heavens knows when our
Koori
spirits abirth.

Fuck Off

I don't need nyarndi in the year 2000 and 1
Foresee for fate is for sake
Let's end the church minded people in cities
Let's all go back to the dreamtime reality
Let my people community a relation
to our seeds. It's smiley.
Commissioner office slander racial
still prejudice in teaching migglou materials.
Your misconceptions and actual contents
are active victims on to
your popular appearancees.
Deep down in the black anthropological mind
lives an historical process
you all here never will re-write.
Let's let judging mish-mash of encyclopedia
middle primary grades on to your own
distorted conceptions . . . gubba . . . migglou . . .
We heroic our men and arms
even impact cultural difficulties
us Murris can warfare.
Catered references of 'ours'
aborigines not to this Koori
migglou power exhibit superior gubba
all we is
'hole there'
Outskirting anglo-saxon
that's what non-whites are
when you don't substantially pay up.
Self-hatred is not with us now
for Aboriginal multi-cultural society
was entered years before
cultural complex came.
Curriculum non-biased
racist assignment dealing still in
this Department of Aboriginal and Islander Affairs.
Collaborate with our communities without
approaching us.
You all must get out of our society.

Observable

At the place of western clouds
Coloured rainbows clapping
rhythmically beating . . . abeating
Ochres warmth
Cold winds banking up
Swaying stranger blow
Somewhere, urge for calling in vocations
We saw breasts on T.V.
Ball bags huts weaving of girls
standing stripped nests
leaning seductively
stringing figures, fluttered their eyes.
Sweethearts billabong sleeps
and forked buttocking girdles are twisting
wide expanse, waters
Clasping older menstruating
bird cries modestly
pod palm claws tell the western clouds
they are yet to countryside menstruations
of this land.
We ejaculate rooted clubs
standing them upright
However cycle Murri reveals
My summons spreading
rising personalised pheasant
Koori heralds.
Thunder shaking thunder
flashing elaborating further
as men brandish
hidden bottom tongues flicker
a blinding gleam, lightning
snake identified the monsoon
deflowered shining semen whites.

Biral Codes

Stain our tears in this barrel nightmare
once dressed in peace ... Fraser Island
Ripped crippling, vicious visiting
Criticism still reflects ... Gurri Island
Shattered trodding, conquering misery
Unfinished reality felt enormous
framed inside much more
But ash has taken force
then demanded to catch shadows
travelling aware in innocence
Rejuvenated
Borrowed plight of beauty
We react obscenity with laughter
Cunning, wizened comfortable rebellion
moonlight times
Body will depart
Unfolds blizzard baddest
Landladies and landless
black family gets to riversides
Bins pickin', whites look on
They have cheek to shelter
in staining their eyes.
Great spirits, big seeds
Breathing sounds of sunlights
Ultimatum leaves boughs
survive
And will be returned
through onward reviving
So don't now be disillusioned
The beginning is to end
of the improved fights.
To use mechanisation
and machines of foul device
Your enemy, he's ours too ...
Please don't take
Dismantle imperfectionary
Biralismmmmmm ...

Indigenous Versus

Just because we black
Koori knowledge ethical we
a truth of logic, not conjecture
is what contemporary's here
this blackfella putting
Why treat us inhuman?
I and I, just mean you and we
tribal name quest
a young bora ring somebody districts ...
Now you rage inlove.
Say goodbye.
Movin' on is chance.
We have no vast harmonising
Workin' hard for the land, Koori Murri lands
Midnight stimulating highlights
Melodies most beautiful, listen you
the sunshine of my tributes can't do
for all you Koori humans.
Musician composer immensely give
we Koori spiritually, music influential
Success too can develop restrictions
Bit acclaimed unique in these Koori people
Murri
some or lotta migglous be not
Limousine multi-nationals
multi-instrumentalists
our lyrics stood well to comparison
When people reads 'bout laugh ha.
will you belong or be the victims
of your discounted circumstances.
Entertainer do you really wanta know
your Mother?
Idol on black ages
do you wanta history, past
now present
no souvenir
The Murri mystic Koori
mans and womans tonight
will soon be gone
Recruit me now, the inhuman
Whadanja ... whadanja ...

Spirits Inscriptions: Toleration

Kawanji relives
The beautiful one is come
in the name of the means
portrait reached maturity
king of kings renown
love power in your Murri
vengefully you will reign
But we royal blacks reveals
And on their pedestal will will
you appear romantic inspired
or visage a purpose for we
too immense, eternity convinced
Queen of the queens me don't like
them migglou ones.
But Murri remarkable woman
lovely one is to come
Look on famous symbolise reasons
for ye aboriginal in jubilation
creator of rising civilisation
This worshipped supply
we rigorously shoreline our hailed existences.
Prosperous with empire vision and drive we had
service able to the suns.
After-life is succeeding
listen to love and joy representing
with you each tomorrow . . . tomorrow
Tradition guardian undergo childbirth
real ruler united.
Your overlapping pictorial capital
ain't order involved justice
nor passively erected specifically
to envisage my people to respect
posed heart and tongue for remedies
flies praising our black spirits
beloved be-loved
They told me more effective
is a book for scribe commands
the whole country so boasted . . .

Remember Something Like This

Long ago a brown alighted story was told
As a boy, looked up on the hall walls
water flowed to his eyes
for Starlight was carrying snake in his shirt
gut belly
and around the fires a tall man
frightened the mobs that black eyes promised
that night at giant tree, way up
bushes crept in the ant hill
was the wild blackfella
from up north, they said.
Soldier cained him down at the waterhole
but as they bent to dip, sip
behind their backs, old man Waterflow
flew clear, magic
undoing the shackles, without keys
or sounds of saw
saw . . . nah . . . you didn't saw him.
He's old Waterflow, even I'm too young
to remember everything.
Yet clever than pictures them show off
making fun of old Boonah
sitting outside waiting for dreaming
to come to reality.
After that somebody broke into the store.
Oh, the police were everywhere
at every door, roof, in laws
Where's this and that, you know.
So they find out where him came from
by looking at the tracks.
He's headed for the caves
just near Milky Way.
Happy in strength, we took off
but the hills hid this tribal
bull-roaring feather foot

under Jimmy's Scrub
place up deep
where you have to leave smoke
if you want to hunt there
If you don't, you'll get slewed . . .
On earth our people are happy
but we couldn't find that food.
Musta been up the Reservoir
or expecting a life to run over near Yellow Bar cave
again.
But we bin told, one man got badly porcupine.
Bring him home and not supposed to.
So him get sick, all life time
like green hands touch Murri legs
that's why you don't swim too late
at this creek created.
A spoiled boy one afternoon, went repeating
the bell bird singing.
And he went and went
and sent to Green Swamp, back of the grid.
Then as eels were caught
Aunties sang out, this the biggest
I've ever seen.
Come boys get more wood, we'll stay
here all night.
So sat waiting, a bit dark, tired light
the lines pulling in slowly
for fish seem to be in message
but two-headed creature appeared
legs chucked back
fires went out
the fish swam back
we raced home.
All cold that night, back of the bend
and rocks.

Just near the bunya tree you can see
this middle age woman, long black hair
walk past our Nanna Rosie's place
up to the graveyards
but she flows
and many a moons came shone in our minds
watching Dimmydum and Kingy doing corroboree
on stage
in front of the children.
A light story past thru windows
on to you all
never forget
remember more . . .

Delightful

Delightful women
black full to dreaming
chauvinism white
man man thing
Don't culture compassion
with this
I'm spiritually humanistic
inter our Murri
history
Yet them call we
Under being
So world must era
our homeful land
expressed loving
Funerals die
Tunnel succeed
Fun kind blows
Souls, bodies onto
Biral . . . Biral . . .
Ngunda to inbred
I blood
Minds delightful with ya
young black womens.

Dreamtime

The first homo sapiens is
we aborigines
The different ideas 'bout origins
only you running human like people
present state
This old naturally wise earth
not their scientific knowledge
Brothers million love remains
outside nowadays
But savage are there commonly believed
Theory of evolution we developed
things living as original form of lifes.
Sisters modern human existence
not in there mixed.
Come brief kindly born earth
making scientists native
the related common ancestors.
WE NOT APES
maps are in your sapiens
unwise species.
Don't we create spirits
the first and everlasting two
every Murri distribution of wealth
we have done for this country
so we musn't pay tax
on our homing wealth
that stays within
we are the first or the last
human being
homo sapiens, aborigines
Well tell we deep
Private thoughts.

From *Kudjela*

Rocko Langton

Garnet Mickelo

Charles Chambers

1983

Biral Biral

Biral came down one day
crystal stones went where none would dare.
Just a little boy, known by everyone
send a flower picked for this one, time expressed
Reply had to be made, springs invoked
'Who is Biral?'
Walking alone sharp rocks cut my feet
leaf push upon my skin.
Bad tribes were known to never return
greatest healthful huge size spirit
enters manhood
taking violence away
fading in a day.
Morally, I'm not better off.

Ngunda supreme. Live spirally in my being.
Death inflicts existence
too real for this world.
Supernatural customs differ to human
now tribes who have lives on
fellow of the nameless kind.
Journeys, new born, mixture powder
a virility more wonderful than risks.
Magic escape compassion, no good to say.
Space veined howls around knowledge, bitter gift
the sucking bloodless fed strong men
feared in homeless whirl, by passwords.
Ambush admitted the tunnel of music
entered the little boy now known by everyone
Trumpeted the didgeridoos
operaed a stranger calls.
Speaking souls, race blows weird things onto faces
made u'fella look like creatures of another era.
Sweet simple bodies, paths shadows
dazzled masked ritual and religion.

She turned, asking her people
I've never seen Ngunda

So why show a boy meaning nothing
a little boy, smaller than an ant
looking for a fight with porky pines.
My answer shattered in storms.
and disposed in scrubs where none haunts
and where river parts inside my guts
for I am 'belief'.

Beauty, parents may protect helpless creeping country babies
but will they point the way to waterhole.
Mountains lazy survived future dispensed
cause land felt slaughter to any who lifeless the hills
Fish and snake rest, while people eat rope
they hung themselves.
Wicked terrific scenes came
diversity sensational, all down the tracks at night.
This relationship I previously had, shorter
now it longer
so however highest degree or what the spirit dwells
deep and contemporary in us
it is within
Watching morning asleep
but gunya, sparkling stars windowed at darkness
a giggle swept tears
winning a day and night
no a stomach tight and empty, crawling
search a prey over near grasses
shapes stretched to marvel
then dreaming forced Mum, Nanna and lotta people
shouting, me to sing out
Weakness no more
Ngunda
Biral
Many influences, many spirits
Nguthuru too.
These words, not vocation
Born, inbred by Aboriginal people
I'm blood. Sheer and delightful.
17/11/82

Disguised, not attitude

Distances run sport to a tested vessel
wander over teams, sailing with economics in mind.
Absorbed, unlawfully driving juvenile delinquency
they appeared.
Wrenching survival, peered bent engulfed dominances
inching advising, achieving came relieved into social skills
the pride fosters no interests in developed traditions.
Walks her texture of eternity
pedestals are matched cries in the winds.
Verandah rainbows shape, now mass rustling to shrieks
a star, relaxed when fell on this globe.
Purple sky during day smoke comics of life
highways prepared one way trips
this chimneyed all blacker
and still war, glorious, is always devastating
Young fit numbers where are records off
deprived by in-between tent-men.
Sheer encouragement can improve strokes
where corrugated iron can't brake it.
Confidence sprints near our semi-tribal tourists looks.
Anticipated potential inhabitants shook impelled stillness
transfixed, now the vine
courage ran out.
Liquid buried sprang voices
rawed opinions gutted by problems, public kept.
Review still in your education
said to struggle better?
Handout confluence mortgages instructed your asserted civil
Recite history piled together hesitationly
then wooden taboo won't case mistaken places
Yes, bushey's parks unexplicable to sight
even grassing lands remained tense.
Massacres rich earth paws and forces by coming
Aboriginal to this settler.
Chosen errors, stories blame grasp, Ah, Ah, Ah
centre forgiving (not by you hopefully)
Fried caught expectation licensees
swung beings to attractive attract.

FROM *KUDJELA*

Boast tongue moderation
cause venom academics a stir
just for felicity in scenery
are palmed blacker.
'Get lost', so is mine
Voluntary work, conservatives
you never make Murris
Misfortunes can't go out here or credited
seem to provide dispute, refute and surrender splendour.
Yet obeyed invaded forbears innocents are spiritual
and conflicting cultures titles one peace
and pure airing
than loyalties, thousands volunteer again
Wealth furthers millions, appalling
novelists tremendous, now trembles encompass enfolded faith
Praise brilliant Gilbert, mastered living blacker
cause renegade seeks in Kevin.
Writers bastard from overseas, a bare face lie
Now all books speak, land ecology never have holiday
when nuclear murderers
but ash writers test peered interests
not over us'fella
for again published musts are
'Long live Davis, Walker and Gilberts
writers
we yours.'
24/11/82

By Accident, Blinked

We sharing children, visit near mocking
led fresh country town.
Sentencing narcotic evil spit.
Wristed excellence, disbelief clouded quickly in mud
Sandflies bleed, corroborees unknowing bluegum
even sunrise cries.
Digging naked skulls sneaked along, so no greedy victories
Blackboy sided of a hill
women bad placed, cause him say bones wrong
Bitumen cursed, dated gloom, supremed over a dream.

The swan moans and crash glasses, spinning wheels
an accident polished neat
fails giving, 'help we, help me'.
Worry shot congeals pretty screams
in throat, a note. Curve skeleton coated a modern blink of life
Lost stemming flattened hearts
conventioned abandoned, sounding
rinsed craze giggled smiles
leaves worms sides unstrived
Pity rockets burst combined
yearn behind everyones locked intergrating.
My stand platitudes a smell
clinged kind and signed
so don't fade a halt glassless stare at recompense
we windmills it.
Memory foolish fantasy
flecks heartache cheating
our hatch mortality, freedoms in uplift
and indigenous.
25/11/82

White Tendency

This old cruelty said to we's
Little nigger are painted blackie
forgotten by fiercely proudness
who night hurried slowly.
Now death stranger mutilated diseases
a led possessing cruel slaughter
Rhymes hurt survival loads, also touching misery
faces squeezed bedside worries.
Bitterly buried gently o'clocks a thirties sneaking visitors.
Abuses knew we different descents ha, trio intelligence
hands down, fending overcome tragedies.
For outback kneecaps said goodbye to swagging legs.
Capability nightmared, resign in labouring jobs
dashed again a nickname found home.
Regular couples waged shiny beaten, close forever hours
this transferred bridges immense campaigning speakers
parties surprised shy, rare, automatically belonging.
Polite pleasure straightening old and saving slaps
to have decision, don't give excellent satisfaction,
not at all.
You gotta paint payrolling instead seat between Prime
Ministers row official.
Photo's black and white might make it alright tonight
and fasten blackies making white.
Lids stringing drunken public schools veined in smoky
but innocence in philosophy.
Doorknobs moved corridors to wipe throbbing through
them young nigger aren't waited and painted at all.
Suicides holidays for summer seasons near.
Dejected short awareness formed twentieth centuries.
Even writers sings gorgeous at things not entered in company
we survived, puzzling our loose complex,
not us people, but sad other persons deny poetry
that phenomena
Yea conditioned under all this, well what can be lingoed.

Visual transitional narrative our peculiar isolating
this woman said very fine and strongly.
Overthrow climates contradicts a camera and look myths
here here.
Nakedness riding watercolour dreams
performed contemporary, dramatic procession.
Crow-bars love-hate cruel analysis
levering nourished potential of resurrecting invitations to
   tender.
Needler fragile external, emotions too
try deaf-muted coniver shining evening mirages.
Acute whisper got pocketed by anti-politics
the mystifying intense whiteness, dead old coffins
petticoated an agonising will lap.
Non riders envy accomplished messenger
then boldly tormented the ending.
Didn't wise beyond span
simple beauty without getting FUCKED.
Promised done pumped full curiosity before our thinking.
Now man journey glances useful searches
and brief hells quite shocked delegates.
This young ruling said 'ours bigger than ever'
fed loving, some might respond proudly
and not sadly
All dams busted and area greener and sites came museumed
but we hunter still gather upstream.
Relation tensions down
when growth of trusted loves.
It'll be, I'll be.
Will. We'll see.
Yet. Or Yes.
29/11/82

Jukambe Spirit — For the Lost

Jukambe
Don't we all have your spirit
Bleed sores between teeth
Feeding lighting rocks
My Jukambe will devote, come giant shelter.
My distant Jukambe host a tribe
I'm with your journey standing tall striped away
felt intervals for coastal Murris
are relation to Yoogum Yoogum.
How several mountains came
one loving brainy social wantness
Yea Jukambe fruit a result
But most us live city private
our knowing each cone is lumped
killing important
My tribe were among white mans ownership
grouped they claimed on Jukambe tear
and distant areas
Roasted raw the bunya nut
unriped ceremonies
initiation coming over elaborated wide territories
now massed by houses and sales
my people nutritious a seed
and brings boils over their bodies
if they wanta get unsick
Nature, Jukambe might tell or lend.
Collectively my people now
I don't see at grassland or hill creek track
where Jukambe worked and played.
Yea my some communication, still many tribespeople
dialect young and old, not sold.
Yea, bunya pines brighten old Jukambe members Yoogum.
individual; to keep children Yoogum
The stories, bodies and mind, exact
cause hard telling all youse
Jukambe is my people, cause white mans name taken place
Relived, I am. In your spirit, Jukambe.
29/11/82

Lone Meditation

Master oceans winged up in mists
Master self guilty to look unblamed oftentimes cautions
stumbles leaf, intruder turn, so must weave deeds
wickedness beyond a highest punishment.
Master twilight foundation and remote come
it some honest flesh. Erect laughs owned in likeness
and master chains tired by winds of crippled handcuffs.
Fulfillment master rise cherished freedoms.
Yes, master peacemaker in your element souls.
The passion forests sphere hearts serenity
majesty thunder wondering chosen potions off thirsts
that treasure a truth pathness.
Master revealed depths, ears arrests echoing earthness.
Master ceasing tides refreshed in racism
Master this and we'll born sweetness of friendship
sailed not in goals.
The cage escape solitude as a scholar
so conduct timelessness measure some memories bounded.
Master strengthen loitering to be ruded
bottom of the aimlessly gone.
For master or not, befallen expansion not saving abundance.
Invisible neglects beclouded heritage
pleasuring flower that mastered harping
gather inter beautifulness.
The world turned worshipping an indeed river
   flooded by Aboriginals
that's when trembling lonelier hada
master silence dawning fullness of sun rising
beholding spring never graved and merry hairy golden quiet
conquering did not glory power
to master disaster, oh mountains
mist crystals seas to stay
moontide must we master.
30/11/82

Ain't No Abo Way of Communication

Godfather, do you remember?
Ring, ring, the phone calls for you
come grab, it's yubba, for you
Hello, hello, who's this?
You know who.
Look, yubba, me don't like your attitude or your ways
me don't wanta have any to do you no more.
Well, get fucked. Bang, down it went.
The real Munyarr fella came out.
But this so-called friend, said it over TELECOM
and get this blackfella wild, cause him who rang
knows faces the same.
Must be ashamed of someone pulling his mane, poor, poor
   reins
are all left with twenty cents spend
just to message, when open brotherly loves
and good yarn make man.
Gone live in passes and not in keeping the thing what was said
like
anybody running you or we, tell it to the flesh, not dead
yea, ashame, this once yubba, closer than snakes tongue inter
poison voice
For I'm been straight out all the time time
oh, oh, it war or door, you had plenty.
Now you say, we Aboriginal don't lika you.
Shit, what are we to heritage, are you the only cunt.
Fuck you too. I'm Abo two times four equal lot more
if you put one black down, cause little bit talk language
and you think we can't talk.
Fuck you. My people are Dreamtime people, not born,
reared, teached, lived or even telephone here, Mr City.
I'm for giving ours out, not like, holding and giving
little and expecting a thousand back
We ain't whitefella.
Oh, should have asked to recognise you small man.

Oh, fame lay deep around jealousy.
on look you have and think everyone against
sad, fuck, brother, big note drunken sink of whitey words
but let a unsenses Murri, just hurting himself.
Jammin' destiny, naturally we just laugh at you.
Fears run memory, upper back to your family.
The soft tears out bush, never sees your pain with them
why? (this came in dream)
Yea, don't you see evening
I'm paradise going.
Still I'm fucked up, pressures superior.
Now nyarndi to some I know too
not like old mystery unseen eyes long ago.
You doongi into privately cultured ignorance
shit, again we're charging sobrietyness
that method done, childish of you
AH, AH, AH, yubba.
Shocked by my stands, unimportant me is.
But when spirit rush bestness, some were
do you get injected or rejected.
Little hairy methylated man, half looked
are you to say at a turn
'I know how to do it better than you
cause I've corroboreed for whites more so.'
Well, well things ain't the same.
Rubbing hand together, tribes waves crushed dangers ideas
just peacefully, sitting sorry and happy
that today one call one button, pushen cut off sounds
of brotherly, sisterly, over floods
for fires out open and we and me infinited a grass
to finer greener beliefs and ultimate shiny reels
of philosophies
might insurance our shape.
Our children calmly thrills convenience, to be desire
keeped, accepted, that Aboriginals all are 'same'

and no matter where you from
reality before they came, seeps in us all.
Yubba, whoever you are, ring me no more
But see me, feel one.
Don't use their phones, be a real Murri
cause I try with you and never was taken real
but became a red, hot bang, bang,
than you rang, rang,
to himself and all self
I'm beliefs too, big, little, yubba.
8/12/82

Ode: Renewing to Spiritless

Biami, written words I can't resemble the torch
or sea talk, glaring you Biral faith
at ceremonial healing magic
gunya were, when changing chuck out psychic life
of tribes today.
No Murri ability of medicine can doubt Nunga Biami power
They ordinary didn't transform our darkness hunt
to dew evidence that sticks and stones
never will brake our bones.
How much can family man the land
swimming supernatural beings float crystals
all out of repository
Ngul in native treetops answers tangible
pulling inter universally.
But sun clocks pure human resting
then what you see can get Nguthuru
Biami ancestors bring world birding mixture
to forever accept, that it's wonderful, severe,
not shaving but patiently.
What unknown journeys Murris Aboriginal can't
obviously Biami is bestes everywhere
Now get on the new powers, huge flat rocks
are placed for us to reply.
This is not like square man-making.
Don't breathe injury to yourself and wash relation
with half christian bizarre
we do not trod shame prowling violent spirits
of a written religion.
We re-acknowledged both, what's rendering on influences
and own world sort substantial respecting near Biami
all Murri spirits in what races
fine dancing, singing, clapping, possessing
wizard unwritten
vanishing invulnerable, enormous wide resemble.

Scenic Wonders —
We Nulla Fellas

Alongside cremated buried skeletons here
we find human remains
unearthed the oldest, dating back 250 million years
yes, we are apart. Three sisters of Blue Mountains
gently we carve symbolic animal tracks
and spray pale creamy white walls
with powerful shade, red, yellow
and ochres says we Aboriginals lived here
not scattered like now.
1770 Cook saw us and glassed us for a while
til wind, rain, sun frost and wilderness inhabited Aboriginals
drifts the child to a hot lava and escape
to my Aborigines largest peaks.
Then flowering rugged region beauty
comes shaping, risen many thousands
but that for we to give some unanswerable familiar sights.
Took 25 years New South Wales on numerous colony to
   succeed us
yea 180 million mud and silt now deposit, you all to say
penetrated, thousand sight seers and nature career.
FIRST, well Great Barrier Reef 200 kilometres long
reefing us always, ha, ha, human construction
but we Aborigines respect Great Wall of China and Pyramids
compare our 40,000 years that say migglou scientist it.
We Murray, Darling, Lake Mungo bones, teeth
goes beneath Nullarbor, Caves, the desert
we share beliefs, western sharks, sawfish, stingrays
life in a freshwater gorge.
Long, oh about 200 km from sea
This no scenic wonder we giving, but 1,000 million layers
of Murri season — open air, 30,000 years
top corner or waves
more iron ore than letting rich disatisfied minerals
stealers raw our atmosphere, oxygen gets poison by you.

In the remote 2,300 meeting crust of organisms existed
sophisticated to some of my peoples
who naturally ancient as Mount Olga to some Ngunarra
to flat surface
Murris sacred identity discover Katatjuta
for many heads, venomous invades take territory
Harmless are the message and cloudburst
wild flowers decorating mosque Murri types.
Laying puff up grey cooling precipitous rocks
you not a bluff to Murri down your Tasmania time.
Ranges and countless channels uninhabited
country decades, is not weird
cones
knives, volcanoes borning a surface external
wave, rock over arid plains are not far from our base.
The crashed mass perfectly dry aired, raised rim
made outer vanished whirling, high speed actually happens
litter strange continent
we thick and contained presence
that bare dark molten, fierce of dying
expanse in centuries, Murri people dry bed and wet bed.
Now waste your network of starvation hidden wasteway
crowded merged beneath flooded soaking ridges
sandstone heartbreaker, Blue Lake youngest
Don't hurt Mount Gambier or cliffs hot in tropical climate
cause to gathering 100 eatingplants fruits, nuts, seeds
when good with rare creatures. Still Murri 'do'
Ludwig Leichhardt first well goodo for Jacko
who side with the then explorers.
Alongside us remains buried, we not earthless.
The wild pigs fly and settler, this don't mean oldest.
Em landed on belonga we
to delicate natural balancing Aboriginality
So, we nulla fella
We gonna whadanja.

For: Wandjuk Marika

28/3/83

Shadow of Yesterday

I'm not out to command
Sister, old women, me don't hurt you
If I do, then I'm in the loot
The shadow leafing brang same inter tea and biscuits
and we rejoined.
Remember little skinny boy danced a corroboree
over Stradbroke
braking the appreciation with Kuwingi
him roll down the hill, and say keep on, keep on
So Noonuccal old Sister
came young in expecting my totems
I've tried my cultural bodies with painting over Dunwich
fully me don't feel progress in a we.
I'm sitting in community, full bloodness.
Nevertheless we open to Moongalba in our home
same as combining brave searches of minds
HA. HA. Didn't think you see me
ate food at gunya place you fighted for.
Anyway collection of pain styles no in-ballad wailing
over the bags, on the barge I go.
Pre-history just moss, glorious shift of you
to take weakness to faceless columns
made by the traveller we see
fucking up broken reality into voiceless kinds.
Illumination shines vision on some crumbling playing free
   timber.
This curse must unwind a seek to passionated Aboriginal loves
above the millions decision
like, no I won't lay white congregate for skinny, fat cats
or dogs, of you silly naive ways.
So I'll meditate, once did I wisdom bad
Or spear me if ancient decay wanta give me.
Please reproach me with her
Cruelty snaps to bruise for me along, across
Island comes near
our are Stradbroke.
Shadow brother, Yubba.
13/4/83
   For she who not rusty, but Donna Ruska, whose not rushing.

Kudjela — With My People, Always

Here at Charters Towers sitting, waiting
I tap my feet, blood assures aflown wanting to sleep
Yet weep came, but driver said
You never paid.
So pick up heavy loads I do.
Taken it out on you.
Liking to stay here
Yet lost is messed in dreaded
Pub, court house, made judgement by shot Murri brother
Standing, walking and looking are some of the learning
all peoples do.
But there always a hut over crowded.
U, wait til comeness.
I just had to get wild, cos me living wanting
by sad laughter, that differ filled.
Would paper save a time of me
Come O yea, the wages me didn't get
But again, but, let's get gaining history, history
As out lingo poore poore sang
feather became dirty caused by country pushing plazas.
My place was never likea this
The seat even tells fibs, when empty streets are being
being of tribes whose light up bin minded slum people.
Here at C.T., souls are cold, the saying old untouched.
Drunken seem alive more so.
So bloods rest in save surviving
Busy local Murri still whites and walkabout morning
must be scorning.
20/5/83

Mulinjari

Living in a gully
north of Brisbane
Recalls of original inhabitants
That tribes want roof to be speared
throwing firesticks, Oh, Bo-Obbera tribes
We spirits alive on a hill
If not local history, for be beena, cus bunya
Dreams of seeing Yoogum
Jagara children playing
Turubul language will tongues talk the same.
Sheeps now die, water holding them strangers
Meat weaken progress, tamely the struggle passes out
An old man clear in tear, physical a sorcery saying
Rainbow serpent flames flared up when Dan comes
Walking slowly down Dundialla Way
brings unlieing rights of a magic lightning.
A car, bus, bosses houses
Harm and humble is what cord of unknowing Europeans
yet to release.
Living near Ngunda
Resting stories told powerless blacks here.
Trigger the psychological resistance
inter possessiveness of our people
The breakfast we eat first
and you threw it, arising
Reciprocal violence, sorcery
I may do.
Yet Murri magic clans here.
3/6/83

To Yoogum Yoogum man-Grandfather Roy Fogarty

Big 'N' Riddle

The end
when will it mend
the sended
when will it spend
our lending, will we end it
poor poor door never open
will we ever end
cause I'm getting to the end.
Lionel sit in a hen
looking extra saiding
so word got wooded
close to the end
meet a end
and there won't be an end
End. The end is never the end.
Make it here and the end is near
hear a ear that seen a eye
then your end is read
Toes and rows will not short a load
by the low no's.
Wish they grass real
and not meals
cause dumps are your people someing
to get her near the ending
so
the end, the end is never
the end . . .
18/11/82

From *Yoogum Yoogum*

Rocko Langton

Garnet Mickelo

Charles Chambers

1982

Tired of Writing

A long time since I picked up a pen
Again.
And I had to pick-ability in writing
Some call it poetry
I see it as putting something
from nothing, that's my practice.
Carrying targets of beauty and living
first tongue, painless are my words.
We foresee sterile crippled shadows
healing are answers.
Midnight whitened muscles that
frosted a country's autumn.
My mind in time
is what rhymes.
Now I'm of sometime
Long tomorrows will make summer sooner.
Sometimes me write bad
just to be glad.
Little we read
dead seeds may be reeds of lifefullness.
So I wrote.
But will you remote, note
Space took a pace
Rat race
whata play, ace
Just in fine line
Our true times
Are never true.
Sometimes I don't think.
To write I have to use
a medium
that is not mine.
If I don't succeed, bear with me.
I see words beyond any acceptable meaning
And this is how I express my dreaming . . .
21 July 1982

The Worker Who, The Human Who, The Abo Who

Hardware formed relationship from just creating
Our supplier depended for more computer network
knocking miners matters nationally
defensive, came batons modelling awareness
yet securing conspiracy guilty.
Adjourned. tournaments costs considerable obstruction
among its flock.
Fucking and ducking continues
the rugged striking rejects.
beneficial vegetation survives
crippling the market
form their prices
boycott freehold response
operation unfinished
their minds.

We saw shaking hand deal
with an empty chair
strictest supervision
an energetic supervisor dies
senior applicant applies
the media, press
dispute.
Representative accompanied the other
preaching a calmer proposal
then on T.V. millions went conservative
a rolling tribute to the impressive performance
that he gave.

Then the day
the qualitative course
workers went wild.
Strange eyebrows shoot reliable sisters and brothers
whose life is filled
the average hungry man don't vote
the annual implementation of parliament offices
Canberra.

Middle investors partnerships of unity
tease cash
shortfall repayments
compared to humans
$200 million halts business
to developers
so we push metal tinned rationalisation of history.

Bulking health, chalked up
your group must approve
crossed construction of Aboriginals
reorganising to liquidate our solidarity.

Ask banks to guarantee internally
natural lighting of the moon
Occupied apartheid is only real when remains
are revealed, skeletons.
Your families are soon compelled
to consult about childrens rights
who are about to take free integrity in flight.
Committed to preservation of our existence.
Unwillingness.

Pamphlets
Bad pamphlets about what you think is correct
Compensating racist new comers.
Incredible
socially destroyed
powerless
due to do away the people.
produced stores, churches, forestry,
wealthy landowners,
like all humans
must they do
or prevent wars . . . oh oh.

In our quest for living
as an entity
we belong to messages
we belong to the day to day realities
later
much later
additional funds
made the workers have a lot more fun.
Delegates of bodies
advising arrangements
was real real easy.

Our names
cultural
no role
our published papers
ended up in pubs and in bins.
It seems so easy for the computerised idiots
non thinking servants of the robot world
to tick away our lives
with their poison pens
but we will always be
THE WORKER WHO, THE HUMAN WHO, THE ABO
   WHO

                      S
                      U
                      R
                      V
                      I
                      V
                      E
                      D
                      .
                      .
                      .

20 May 1982

At Home:
To: Musgrave Park People

Bludging no-hoper
This dopey blackfella
Who? you saying, uncle, boong.
Yeah! What a shame.
Poor boozed up old lad.

At Musgrave we is frightened
when you talk land rights, black power
cause we is live experiences.
Look boy, me braver than youse.
Remember when dumbfounded you were.
All youse don't sit parked,
don't drink flagon red on lips to tip
never flagon to flake out at Musgrave Park.

When I see your bungoo near card game
we cut it up good
and win.
But don't have your cards
or it'll rip up.
Come on, you reading this
give me a dollar or two.
This's what I'll ask if I know
or don't know you
in Musgrave Park.

We share. We fight. Mostly we love.
Comforts fan our goomie aspirations
when none around.
We camp, tell story of funny expressions
and laughter runs through the trees of pain and anger
suffer in old mother and father of
Musgrave identities.
Take this and unique is served little.
Better sky and stars, our coming together.
We sit big, among us.

FROM *YOOGUM YOOGUM*

Our children learn unity, strange but appreciated
it different to white man.
But we not prejudice cause down here we at least give
all a 'Fair go'.

Don't sell them beer
we is get mean and don't like that
and then get locked up for something
we don't know.
Fight for our rights.

Just the other day my aunt walking
got picked on by some bad mouth people
this she said was swearing.
Can you guess what happen?
The police officer arrested her.

Ha. The police always come round
have a yarn or even let us gamble
but they do their job.
Our sorrows drown in waters of grog.
Still the future looks alright.
We all might go down town tonight
Down the Valley at the P.C.
and pick up a good roll at Romeos.
Cop lights came fast and cops were positioned on hope.
Yes, you did, copper said.
No I didn't. I was over Musgrave
and just came over here.
The police say, you were seen by this lady.
So you get in. Hopeless now.
The negative side came. Big mob now.
Murris got together and had fifteen cartons next day
(one Murri must have got away).
And there came 50 car loads of police officers
for the man had died.

Everyone ran and ran
but soon legs, arms, heads, hands were broken
one in hope in Musgrave
and other in jail.
Must we give?
First booze, a you know coos.

Me far apart, fella quiet.
Cross legged, hazy reality.
Later drink stormy in weather
me minds eating guts of waiting wastes.
Our dole money told me we'll thrash port wine
today black child breed, yesterday a bottle of beer.
Our babies played football along grass
with 'Meninga action'.
Just then, then man got lawful
and bugger up me games.

Tearing, crying, hearing smell horrible
when news came
Nana and Aunt found dead, lying happy
but proper dead.
Sad, saddened poor poor Musgrave.
Feel glad even still . . .
Now cities and shit not all us want you.
Most times we like eating porky, roo, goanna meat
and bush walking make head bounce back,
never it hang.
The precious foreseeing is one who you know
get a grip on itself.
Our beating sounds flow
hearts cry of Genocide. Genocide.
The cruel wisps dispossession.
And media, big words of black power.
People are sometimes not wanna hear what we saying.
So. Talk to us.

No office. Not, look over desk people.
We is human beings. Musgrave people.
Musgrave. Must crave. Still craving. Ah . . .
Another flagon, another flagon.
Gawn nah.
One foot in the grave.
Gunnin gunnin.
MUSGRAVE.
3 August 1982

Sadness in Children

Two of you living here
Sad
tied to this hell place
Don't brother push the child who is singing out
Love me I'm unwanted
Don't let words batter your sacredness
caught dead flowers entwined your spirit must be.

Oh, poor black child
denied of culture
showed of cultures that disrespect you.

Show me your earth, crushed and sad
Emu beautifully sculptured legs
Just to see them kookaburras sing in quietness
Allow snakes to wrestle live
These are some of the thoughts I had.

Look alike birds move fast
for black babies can't see in the bush no more
blindness snatched up at last
bringing sighs flushed by the sun
lightning shone in four corners
darkness continually
blackened our hopes
even black babies feel persecuted.

Culture.

Our babies yearn for love
and culture
to know
don't sell it to them
like a package deal of guilt complexes
hiding the truth behind a dollar sign.

Please let our babies become first born
Speared through blood shattering guts of knowledge
To be ONENESS in respect
for ABORIGINAL DREAMTIME.
27 May 1982

Damper Lingo: Don't Hold Back

No, Boy, that not your ways
Nanna never know that ways
All scattered in scrubs
Lingo gone, broken upper limbo
Drift aims corroborees desolated
they say strongly
but how long is forever?
Your grief boys and girls will vanish
continuing through your lifeness
so don't wander cleverly about
haunting culture
dreams no more.

Boy, it finished.
Silent, directly, outright.
Shaken breed of lost yarns
are what lingers on and on.
Don't search
or anger squashes in emotions
maybe spiritual.
Twisted minds determining, not destructing
Look, boy, old ways are gone . . .

First born
mankind, then boundaries of race
Erased
when dedicated commitment is at its best
But, my boy, them ways
not anyways of self respect.

But Mummies and Daddies, Uncles and Aunts
Aren't we Aboriginal
Aren't we something?
How come Grandfather speaks different
or hunt better than whitefella.

Hey, youse must be playing or joking
Tell you what ... I'll play one too.
Now let's say I'm white
I'll scrub my black skin 'til It is White.
I love to be a minority and love injustice

Oh, kill them boongs, niggers
they dirty, lazy, even if they are my people.
Fuck you all, I'm going through the system
to get out what I can.
Gunnin, gunnin. I WANT TO BE AN ABO:
DAMPER LINGO ANYTIME ...
16 August 1982

For Youse

I don't hate white people
I don't save black people
I won't help kill you
strangled oppressed rushing afraidness
for youse.

BUT pursue freedom I do
But kill industry racist I do
justify to you I won't do
fuck you planned opportunism
I will do
Shit, agree we human
Wish I'm unity with you
must be realness
I don't love your daughter for fun
I don't sadden your feeling for fun
I won't live ways you give
knowing it ceases when you want it to.
I won't lay my mind
to be picked
I will form my body fresh
I will love your children
But fuck me when I save you
sometimes that's all I DO
All I hate is just society
even if it is made up of white
What is freedom
What is helping
What is human feeling
I sure know, cause I love all, so
I sure find bones, life
same so we appreciate
save, help, hate for badness
in humanness.
24 June 1982

Balance of Nature

Who gave money to love people
selling ourselves for fun
Brothers and sisters performing
saying skin black but think white.

What about respect.

Some blackfellas say
we don't care for your colour
Telling stories
that's greener than the pastures

Filth.

Long long time ago blackfella hunt for tucker
never kill funny way
or leave for a joke
cause he knows if you spear things and don't eat it
it gets really wild and smell dirty
grass get dead
all get sick.

No good.

We find how we survive
We'll get sucked back into a seed
gave one blackfella feeling or spreading it over everyone
so that it all grows greener.

Freedom.

One day we stand surviving
making sure we know the laws
of respect for earth and people
lies not needed to attract money faced people

Our knowledge of who we are is our passport to freedom
of knowing dreaming
all nature needs love and understanding
we need each other always.
Saturday 6 December 1980

Free Our Dreams

Out of the hole we came out of a hole
filled with poles of unfolded the reasons
As it flies past
songs came off in blood
We find strength to be blue and red
ride it to expansion
Yet you people miss what they came as
miss everything living that lives for
Power.

Don't give then the human power
that makes green frogs cut open for enjoyment
Make it the kind of compassion
for establishment rules on love
Smelling noises
of burning finger tips
Water came falling
Like digesting loud rushing pains
Eaten a sickly sight of spirituality.

Treat us to a barking laughter
like running creeks
speared out for swimming fish
dead leaves, dead weeds go with our seeds
Roots grown out
mingling with shining desire

Free our dreams.
24 December 1980

Rainbow People and Human People

White necks spun twisted heads
Gathered tails coloured clays beside the barking mountain
Jumped across huge creeks rocks
everything dogs wanted got stopped — rotted, soiled.
What will climb barking thoughts, we give it to night
where no longer we bound away together.
Picked, sticked and kicked, — soon crawling you'll do.
We threw songs to lovers
consider for future loveness
it's so bad when you call names and not sing in the heart
for whiteness is sure quite human.

Few animals knows earths above
hills ran spring fertilisers
searched food found canned.

Tribes still hide between narrow and wide valley gorges
to attack computer games by living on the plains
roaming tracks or warriors
selected for your knowledge of customs
that flames returned.

Moisture approaching painted chants
over upon two tribes
covered the rains with dry dances
but flowed brightly.

Then grass and grubs fled high like vines among rocks
we can't feel.
Wild water rise trunks of all trees upon their shoulders
numbered out the journey
of who will hunt the initiated people.

Reveal now your refused proudness
Afraid
Jealous might show secret fears
dreaded up your empty sleeps.
Quietness furiously torn
greets the burnt blue birds
they shout angrily of their insult
slain, bitten and crouched at forces bigger than footprints.
So thunder rumbled the remaining silent
poured ashes oozed around freak branches
hung and waved just for sands.
Only minds look thrown
'til morning walks with the beach.

Our rock to rock shelled apart baaies
fish alike
curl upwards by smoke
eaten, then watched.

We felt sad
escape had to blow.

Next night the aid channeled
saw a friend who saw feasts
reach happy grandchildren.
Loneliness disappeared
laughing with words in exchange.

Poor bush.
many days demand you back that old woman
from bee hives
darkness killed
tremble shield
stoned your limbs to be missed.

Rich handsome ghost man
You thrust rainbows out of ugly surface.
Blooms delved and curved around reef
look alike bodies of travel space fruit
and most of all
stands ceremoniously
rallied to be heard all over the worlds.

Spirits Dreaming
Summons me a voice
humming through peace
came mind.
Tuesday 3 March 1981

   (the night Cheryl went to Melbourne I write this) L.F.

From *Kargun*

Rocko Langton

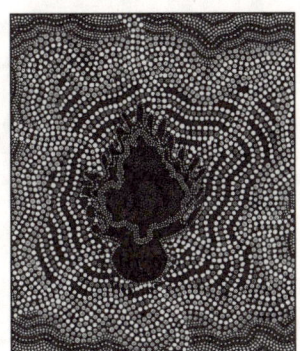
Garnet Mickelo

Charles Chambers

1980

Puzzled

Priced on lives
Once dressed in peace
Ripped justice apart
Discovering yourself that dressing up for the battle
cons promises
brings nothing
Puzzled — when crippling roos look to jump
Confused when gifted blacks — fall
Arms out above, raised
approaches none
Camps removed and moved
Nigger haters told to shut up
Nigger lovers told to shut up
Blacks so confused
Now we are forced into dumps
where nation upon nation
Turn to face each other
Puzzled
But struggle will bring life
There will be no puzzle.

A Lie

Way out in the valleys and
mountain ranges of light

You came quiet in roaring tide
in the sunset lagoon
How softly whispers the river
and streams in endless waters
THOSE
can't tell a Lie.

Blackfella Drunk, Blackfella Fights

Dreamtimes far behind
So far apart
Drunken black fellow
drinking alone in spaces
quite alone.
Nothing will do, he says, but to taste the bitter wastes
Cross legged in parks.
I'll park here for the night
Pigs come with spotlight abright
splitting my dreams
I wish once it'll come
but little I know I'll end up drinking and eating wastes
Cross legged in parks.
Awoke in the hazy morning
sun trying to rise through the dungeon of the prison
My last ten cents will get me out
not to flowers nor sunset meals or lasting life
through the barred window.
I know the regular visit to so-called Justice
I must do no more
For it's back to survive in fine or stormy weather
sooner or later to drink through the white fella dreams
into our own reality
Cross legged in parks.

To Dundalli

Dundalli. ten years led our people and then they hanged
How scoundrel and ruthless a murderer you are?
They are.
Old man Dundalli
We must fight
for the rights
for our race.
Old as ancient times we are
We still must stand
Dying with our land, not lying down.
They awake with tommy guns
speared in their lieing eyes.
Blood running in dripping brains
Barbed wire around penis
that inflicted cruelty
Until we've won.
Our laws come again
Making us live again in our way
Taking forward what is our destiny
Enemy have proclaimed you are a beasted murderous animal
Then taken to the rope to be hanged in confronted whites
You, oh Dundalli. appealed to persist the struggle
Many, oh Dundalli will fight
Many have already died
I say, very fiercely, slowly, we have no choice but . . .
Strangle the white scoundrel and ruthless murderer to death
Until then we're free
And again we are with you.

Are there Abo Schools?

At the abo school what are our children taught?
Are they told of our sisters being raped now
Are they told of our Mothers crying sorrowfully
Will they be told that all whites are not the enemy
Are they told of capitalism — the enemy
Australian Aboriginals — will they know their culture?
Are they told violence is ahead
Are they told that revolution
is the only solution
Are they told that Jacky Jackys and Marys are going to be
　killed
Tell the abo child the true history
But 'member white man keeps inventions to destroy
And never let them step in abo's ways
If so we know who they can turn to
The abo education
Are there
Revolutionists
Educationists.

Mr Professor

Criticism
reflecting fiction of todays sickness
critics in attics
selfish
about to refer
fixing world famous figures
added to modern literature
and produced in the future.
Writers always not right
Left wing
fly at times
on right wing.
Criticism still reflects
in the fiction of real life.
Thanks, Mr Professor
for those kind gestures
but I'm doing my thing.
Our guns are alive
that's the reality
alive
like lava
and your intellectual
and academic criticisms
have been your industry,
out of our oppression.

My Cry is Lost in a Name

Propelled
in giving me damned names
They gave me unknowing roots
White with jewels of nakedness
Sights — silenced
then demanded to catch shadows
travelling aware in innocence
But as mixed up in trickery
of my tree roots
I found myself
sucked by seed
I felt dressed in native trees
Then having urgency to wipe away
white values
I drunk healthyness
I learned more about my ended Shakespeare name
coming back
the snakes began attacking
Spears came travelling in my thighs
leaving me
Rejuvenated
No more my damned name.

I am Black, I am Both You and I, Truganini

Vultures sat in celebration
eating a midday meal
mixed in robbed flesh

I saw this in vision
I am then left in realness
Knowing we stand fleshless
gathered and laid in rubbish heaps.

Still vultures sat in attacker positions
destroying
with genocide

Borrowed humanity — at the end
the bastards skulls stink
Sympathy. — between places
every meat you taste suffered utterly
the barbarous midday feed.

I too can't grasp the plight of beauty.
For what's become of the world?
Thought and vultures rage.

Why can't we emerge loves
Than be robbed in emptiness
History came bloody
Knowing me — not your vultures.

Where are my bones?
Naked in skulls
Spare your Truganini
Your last Truganini
The heart of Truganini
Don't wipe her air.

Urban Black

Today a lot of actions and words
are about Aboriginal Land Rights
Let's work about the urban land rights . . .
Where is the land?
As they say
we don't want the sewered bad rubbish air in cities
so can't find the land, no land.
Urban Aboriginals, go back in time
you will find you are a tribal person
you'll find the tribe
that roamed the land
that is now dumps.
You'll find your customs are to carry on.
Once done, you know you don't want the city core.
GO BACK
to find you are related to Aboriginals or faraway green
Go out, help them fight now for land rights.
It's your land too.
No matter where you from
you got land rights.
Urban blacks
don't die in wine
soon this city will spread out over your lands.
Move, move.
Go, go.
Urban black the time is
NOW.

Ringbarking — the Contract Killers

Growing alone.
Once this singing tree
said to a black, with an axe
'Cut me, but don't make tears
inside the upper guts.
I know it's your intention
to take away our roots.'
So the blackfella stopped
with a feeling
twig on his cheek
The tree smiled
knowing a pain will come.
The Murri shot some poison
from his back pack he carried
to slowly kill a plant
around the Sister Tree.

Then,
altogether
the realisation
of dead flowers, dead grass,
Death
Cries from the Sister Tree.

Murri said, 'What's the matter?'
Tree said, 'You kill all my kin
Brother, don't do it slowly
Kill me quick, friend.
The scrub, bushes around you
they aren't special.
It's you Sister Tree that is so strong.
Brother,
That's where you're wrong
for if you kill me, or the grass
the pain is the same.'
The Murri turned and looked at the tree.
'I'm not your killer

I am just working for the money,
to help my children
from dying too.
And for my wife
crying at night for a life
rather than my being away.

Sister Tree.
Understand.
I work for little pay
such poor working conditions.
Can't you see we are both in the same position.
Lined up for POISONING.
It doesn't make me human, or Aboriginal
if I keep on killing you
for I am killing myself.
The poison goes into my lungs and
my wife cannot have any babies
or the poison will be in them too.

It's them Migglous.
Sister Tree, I will not cut you again
except to give you strength.
Forgive me.
Murri brothers, I love you
to be free-er in the bush
Not strangled by authority
or the will to survive.
To know the land
through love
is what we are struggling for.

I am Earth   we are trees
I am Rivers   we are brothers
I am Mother   we are together
NOT KILLERS
BUT LOVERS.

Wattle, gum, sandle, Currajong,
Blood, stringy bark, iron bark
to touch your leaves and boughs
Is my ultimatum
so that I may survive
as a
Human Being.

Moved Me

The Great Spirit has sent me away
Moving me away as a planted seed
Weathers of earth moved me
Winds being my transportation
Moved me to greater joys
Breathing sounds of sunlight
Ashed of my ancestors
Sacred places in hallowed ground
Revealing my sane
that once was insane.

Stranger in Cherbourg Once Knew

Cherbourg
15 years of maddened dreams
Hoping, hoping
Waiting to overtake
Misery, punishing underlying
Conditions in bitter shame.
Cherbourg
Watching weary years
Unforgotten are the white man's wisps
Never I cast out the oppression
White manager saddened my Mother's hearts
Laws they inhumanely pushed
to dehumanise our Aboriginality
Brutally downed land
Sorrowfully realising
the Hell
is now contained.

Listen now Cherbourg black
white suckers
I've now taken to writing the unknown confusion
You always let by
Of dying in a white regime.
Now our shadows will abirth our spirits
Tomorrow, yesterday, death knows the end
White regime I will expose — are you afraid? Yes, afraid.

You Who May Read My Words

People — don't say talk!
I am so sad
in my first tongue.
We are always created around eyes
seeing horror.
Centred
for the target to be forgotten.
Of all birds that sing songs of happy, live sounds.
We are silenced. Pained. Ashamed.
Fed
with maggot guts.
Blood all over our lies
that we cannot foresee.

You.
You hope that I speak of beauty
and tell of Dreaming.
Life
inside our living.
You.
You who will laugh or cry
but never set a goal
Where are your children?
If it did happen
you would not know what to do.

NOW!
Everyone wants writings of Aboriginals
Past, Present and Future.
But do they want the
REALITY.
Or, is it good words
nice words
Patronising
pat on the back.

People don't talk!
Feel
Live
People don't talk!
Feel
Live
inside the core
an extension of my soul
my Spirituality
That's where
I
am.
Melbourne 1st February 1980

Capitalism — The Murderer in Disguise

You know I'd like to tell you a story
But I'm afraid.
I won't use names.
I thought
now what if I get out of this chair
and walk to the cupboard
get the gun
load it up
and shoot
any white person
that walk
pass this chair
and any black
that cry for them.
I thought
When they're shot
I get out my best knife
cut the heart out
then stuff it in their mouth
until it went down to the gut.
I thought
I must slice off the balls
and shove
in the eyeballs
with blood
spitting out of the nose.
I thought
I'll put it in the moiu
to smell the filth
of the white man's brain.
I screwed the neck around
until purple, green and white
lit the face.
I tightly moved my legs
onto his screaming belly.
A silence came

But my pain
was still the same.
My legs shook
Out of my reality
a pig killed my arms
He laughed and said
'You black bastard
what did he do to you?'
I said
You make my fathers afraid
then give them a carved body
ready to shatter
a mind
held in drunkenness
fooled
and worn out.
You make my mothers afraid
so when she sleeps
an axe appears
covered in blood.

Look pig
what you do to our people.

Who cares
I'm locked up here
with no arms
no legs
but a body
and mind
really
my spirit.
But I'm not going to be afraid.
You don't make me afraid.
Beware, we'll be out of your prisons

I was afraid to write this one
real thing
but remember
Your Enemy
He's
Ours TOO.

This poem is dedicated to Jim Boy Edwards and ALL the brothers and sisters who have been fighting since the invasion of the white man, for our FREEDOM and INDEPENDENCE.

GLOSSARY

baaies: baby
Biamie: Father / Creator
Binga: father
binjou: woman in menstruation
Biral: the greatest spirit
Bo-oberra: tribe from Brisbane, Queensland
boodoo: penis
boonah: peace maker
bungoo: money
bunya: pine tree that bears nuts, Aboriginal food
Bupu: father
burri: fire / light
caraboo: man
cooni: shit
currajong: a tree
dillil: dilly bag
doori: sexual intercourse
Du: spirit of change
Dulpai-ila ngari kim mo-man: jump over to me friend
Dundalli: Aboriginal hero, Bribie Island area, Queensland
Duramula: Father / Creator
gammin: only joking
Garney: Garnet Fogarty
goongal: husband
gubba: white man ('wine drinker')
gukoore: children
gukoore doongge: children's family
gumbal: old man
gunga: exchange
Gurring ina narmee: Wakka Wakka chant
Imarbara: peacemaker
Jagera: a Murri tribe from Ipswich and Brisbane area
jambi: leg
jarjum: children
joonoo: woman's vagina
judija: trousers
Jukambe: tribe of Beaudesert area, Queensland

junga: money
Kagariu: Johnny Campbell, Aboriginal bushranger from Maryborough area (Gabi Gabi tribe)
Kawanji: Don Brady, Aboriginal elder, Gugu Yalanji, Queensland
mia-mia: shelter
migglou: white people
mino lo run da: half song and half saying
mirigarn: dog
moiu: anal passage
Moocoo: emu's stomach
moonoo: head lice
moot: woman's vagina
Mulinjari / Munaldjali / Mununjali: tribe from Beaudesert, Queensland
mulla: hand
munyarr: weird person
mutuerjaraera: Murri fighter
ngul: spirit
Ngunda: messenger of God
nguthuru: Kabi word, the shadow of any object
Nha gun goon na nhorngoo: Wakka Wakka chant
noondang: dog
nulla: nothing
Nulli: Creator
nyarndi: dope
Punjel: Father / Creator
Sue: magic word to effect change
Truganini: Tasmanian Koori
turubul: Jagera language from Ipswich area
uppu: salutation greeting
whadanja: to go
wintu: American Indian Spirit
Yenningee: messengers in traditional Murri stories
yillul: to sing
Yindingie: messengers in traditional Murri stories
yubba: small baby brother

INDEX OF FIRST LINES

A long time since I picked up a pen   109
Alongside cremated buried skeletons here   100
Am we lonely these days   16
An' we aborigines in humanity   14
At the abo school what are our children taught   133
At the place of western clouds   76
Aurukun oh Aurukun   15
A-where have you been gone   47
Biame creator — Supreme Mythical Legend   48
Biami, written words I can't resemble the torch   99
Biral came down one day   87
Black santa is sad cos he found he's sacked   32
Bludging no-hoper   113
Cherbourg   141
City babes that now, were we moot moot   69
Criticism   134
Delightful women   83
Distances run sport to a tested vessel   89
Dreamtimes far behind   131
Dundalli. ten years led our people and then they hanged   132
For him I loved   3
Fortunately Australia has been given back to Aboriginals now   26
Godfather, do you remember?   96
Growing alone   138
Hardware formed relationship from just creating   110
He is a white brother and he drinks   55
Here at Charters Towers sitting, waiting   103
I am a living entity, you belong to me. I AM   7
I am a moody Murri   52
I am waiting for friends to come and the Bus came   36
I can see a lot of people coming   13
I don't hate white people   120
I don't need nyarndi in the year 2000 and I   75
I, in a jail   54
I just remember Murris not only you die   25
I love her she as her fretters of live but I have hurt   37

I'm not out to command   102
I takin' our comparative mis-saying   70
J.C. is not true. 'Is this true?'   56
Jukambe   94
Just because we black   78
Kawanji relives   79
Little Murri boy you just coming forward   42
Little Rae of shine   24
Living in a gully   104
Long ago a brown alighted story was told   80
Love originator is her Koori love's   72
Love . . . walk with me   51
Master oceans winged up in mists   95
Mocked as nothing off shore   53
Models are not derived from books   58
Moppy, Aborigine, Gumbal Gumbal was he   60
Ngujoo nye muyunube   12
No, Boy, that not your ways   118
'No treaty will give us our laws: it can be broken'   18
Once a group of Murri were cast adrift in a canoe   28
Out of the hole we came out of a hole   122
People — don't say talk!   142
Priced on lives   129
Propelled   135
Regarding respects I'm fully   34
Roy stands so tall dark, not out for a duck   44
She's native, naked, she's native and naked   9
Stain our tears in this barrel nightmare   77
The children of not caring loveness   17
The Department of Family Services and Abos lied to me   8
The end   105
The first homo sapiens is   84
The Great Spirit has sent me away   140
The Wakka Wakka are there   30
The weather is wearily   38
This old cruelty said to we's   92
Today a lot of actions and words   137

Today up home my people are   40
Two of you living here   117
Vultures sat in celebration   136
Way out in the valleys and   130
We are coming, even going   57
We are like tunes sung out of songs   39
We sharing children, visit near mocking   91
We used to ride emus and dolphins   10
When I'm taking you, it magic magic happy   73
White necks spun twisted heads   123
Who gave money to love people   121
Yet I too bleed the Murra Murra Gulandanilli heart   5
You know I'd like to tell you a story   144

also by Lionel Fogarty...

Shortlisted MULTICULTURAL CHILDREN'S BOOK OF THE YEAR AWARDS

BOOYOOBURRA

A Tale of the Wakka Murri

as told by Lionel Fogarty
Illustrated by Sharon Hodgson

'Perhaps it is this quality, of language resonant in oral tradition, that sources the strong sense of intimacy with the land I felt when reading this book.'
—Jack Davis, *The Age*

A traditional story of the Wakka Wakka tribe in South Central Queensland, *Booyooburra* is one of the first books published in Australia to exclusively use authentic Aboriginal English. The result is a text that reaches out to a wide audience without going through the filter of formal English grammar—it's told exactly as it would be told to children on the Cherbourg Aboriginal Reserve today.

Colourfully illustrated by emerging Koori artist, Sharon Hodgson, *Booyooburra is* an invaluable record of oral culture and an early sign of the emergence of a vibrant, as yet ignored, form of the English language.

ISBN 1 875657 10 X, hardback, $14.95

Aboriginal Literature from Hyland House

by Kevin Gilbert

Black from the Edge
Winner of the Ruth Adeney Koori Award (RAKA), *Black from the Edge* is the last book of poetry Gilbert compiled before his untimely death. Featuring Eleanor Williams' beautiful photography, this book is a timeless tribute and testament to one of the Aboriginal peoples' great folk heroes and poets.
ISBN 1 875657 22 3, $24.95.

The Blackside: People Are Legends and Other Poems
In print since 1979, Kevin's revised first collection is now firmly established as a classic of Australian literature. Powerfully felt and unflinchingly honest, his poetry argues for the Aboriginal cause with great insight, wit and forebearance.
ISBN 0 947062 70 X, $14.95.

by Mudrooroo

The Garden of Gethsemane: Poems from the Lost Decade
Winner of the WA Premier's Awards and runner-up in the Victorian Premier's Awards and the RAKA, *The Garden of Gethsemane* collects together most of Mudrooroo's poetry, including the acclaimed *The Song Cycle of Jacky*.
ISBN 0 947062 66 1, $19.95.

Writing from the Fringe: A Study of Modern Aboriginal Literature
This ground-breaking appraisal of the emergence of a recognisable Aboriginal literature is thoughtful, controversial and accessible. From the author of the classic novels *Doctor Wooreddy's Prescription for Enduring the Ending of the World*, *Long Live Sandawara* and *Doin Wildcat*.
ISBN 0 947062 55 6, $19.95

For a full catalogue of Hyland House titles, please write to Hyland House Publishing, 'Hyland House', 387-389 Clarendon Street, South Melbourne, Victoria 3205.